▼ ▼ ▼ ▼ ▼

MAKING REAL WHAT I ALREADY BELIEVE

▲ ▲ ▲ ▲ ▲

To Rod & Cathy

[signature]
CalvinCrest '99

*Of All the Things
I Believe As a Christian,
What is Really Mine?*

MAKING REAL WHAT I ALREADY BELIEVE

JOHN FISCHER

BETHANY HOUSE PUBLISHERS
Minneapolis, Minnesota 55438

Published by Bethany House Publishers
A Ministry of Bethany Fellowship, Inc.
6820 Auto Club Road, Minneapolis, Minnesota 55438

Printed in the United States of America

Library of Congress Cataloging-in-Publication Data

Fischer, John.
    Making real what I already believe / John Fischer.
       p. cm.

    1. Fischer, John. 2. Christian biography—United States.
3. Christian life—1960–   I. Title
BR1725.F49A3 1991
209'.2—dc20
[B]   91–18872
ISBN 1–55661–138–2   CIP

To all those who are
seeking to make real
what they already believe.

JOHN FISCHER is a veteran of the American evangelical culture. A pioneer in what has come to be called contemporary Christian music, he has performed as a concert and recording artist for over twenty years. As a speaker and Christian songwriter, he is known nationally for his desire to stir Christians to understand their faith and to live it out in their culture. For several years his insightful columns in *Contemporary Christian Music* have been a favorite monthly feature.

More recently, John has also become known as a bestselling author. His books *Real Christians Don't Dance!* and *True Believers Don't Ask Why* have helped many discover the *essence* of their faith. As a seminar speaker he specializes in basic Christian growth, the arts, and the single life.

He and his wife and children make their home in California.

All of us have become like one who is unclean,
and all our righteous acts are like filthy rags;
we all shrivel up like a leaf,
and like the wind our sins sweep us away.

For as the days of a tree,
so will be the days of my people.

Isaiah

Preface

If you cannot express yourself on any subject, struggle until you can. If you do not, someone will be the poorer all the days of his life. Struggle to re-express some truth of God to yourself. . . . Go through the winepress of God where the grapes are crushed. . . . struggle to get some expression *experimentally*.

Then there will come a time when that expression will become the very wine of strengthening to someone else. But if you say lazily—"I am not going to struggle to express this [truth] for myself, I will borrow what I say,"—the expression will not only be of no use to you, but of no use to anyone. Try to state to yourself what you feel implicitly to be God's truth, and you give God a chance to pass it on to someone else through you.

Always make a practice of provoking your own mind to think out what it accepts easily. Our position is not ours until we make it ours by suffering. The author who benefits you most is not the one who tells you something you did not know before, but the one who gives expression to the truth that has been dumbly struggling in you for utterance.

> From Oswald Chambers' *My Utmost for His Highest*, December 15th reading, read on the morning I completed the manuscript for this book. JWF

Contents

Unknown to me, the maple tree bestowed its wisdom six times. Six years I raked and bagged its sacrificial offering and never saw it. Now, the seventh time, it is unfolding all six years before my eyes. Not that I couldn't have seen it earlier, it's just that I didn't see it in the full scheme of things. I was too busy raking to hear the message in the falling leaves.

Introduction

There is a process by which we come to own what we believe. It's the process of asking the question, "Is my faith truly my own or is it borrowed, second-hand, a parroting of truths others say they believe?"—and asking that question as often as it takes, at deeper and deeper levels, until you have the answer that rests on the bedrock strata of your soul: "Yes, this faith is *mine*." It's a process that must come for us all, but perhaps especially for those who have grown up in a Christian environment, or for those who have been Christians long enough to wonder whether it is Christian networking or their own inner faith that keeps them believing.

I can imagine other cultures and other times when "owning your faith" wasn't an issue, as it is today in the western world. In a season of persecution—for instance, as in the early church—ownership of faith is not something you contemplate, not something you write a book about. You don't wonder about your faith when you are serving time for it in prison: you sing hymns in the night. In a persecuting environment, faith bears a heavy price: no one risks their life, social position, or well-being for a faith that is only easy words, picked up while living for some time in a Christian sub-culture.

The book of *Acts* is, as its name plainly states, a book about the action of faith. These people acted immediately on their faith. They took huge risks to believe. Often, they acted before they fully understood what it was they were doing. Swept up and carried by their faith, they acted first and read about it later. If you stand in front of a lynch mob to give an account of your faith, you can be sure that you will have crossed the line of ownership—if not before, at least by the time you open your mouth to speak.

Today there are no lynch mobs after us western believers. (Some have recently tried to claim "martyrdom," but unfortunately they've been under attack for reasons other than the gospel.) Instead there are warm, tolerant, sympathetic bodies of supporters eager to applaud the faintest testimony. Today, we Christians are so filled with teaching I believe our greatest danger is that we are too full to act. It's easy to become so mired in dogma that you render yourself incapable of doing anything other than attend one more seminar to sort it all out.

This Christian faith: *Where is it—what is it?*

There is a faith that we carry alongside—it comes as part of one's background and heritage, and even geographical location. There is also a faith that's a part of one's social commitments—a part of the expectations of family, friends and community. There is a faith that may have begun with loving action out in the real world, but has since become only a protective reaction *against* the world. Another faith may have only become subservient to, and carried along by, the powerful influences of belonging to a group. Yes, there is even a faith that will benefit one's career, opening up a "born-again market" to the sanctified services of a Christian business or profession.

And then there is something altogether different—a faith that springs within the heart, and runs in the veins. This faith is as strong alone as it is in a group; it thrives in death or in life, in joy or in sorrow; it remains the same whether it brings gain or loss; in fact, it does not calculate the cost but gives itself wholly to its Object; it drives and motivates all by itself. This faith is never "carried alongside"; it is the thing doing the carrying. This is the faith that I write about.

Is faith, for you, a possession of immeasurable worth? Have you wrestled with it until it's so much a part of you that no one else can wrestle it away? Is yours a faith strong enough to mold the world, instead of molding to the shapes around it? Are you an expert on it, or do you need someone else to explain your faith?

According to the Psalmist, the man or woman of faith will be like a tree planted by the waters, yielding fruit in season. But we know that, for the tree, it is not all "green leaves and summer." We contemporary western Christians want a set of beliefs that always yields fruit in ways that are external, measurable: We want *benefits*. But faith is more like the sap that sustains the tree through all of its seasons. It is *life* at the deepest-down levels. Faith is what makes you alive, not because you live shielded in a Christian "forest," but because your roots have taken hold in good soil. This faith is sometimes lonely—but always abiding and true.

This book is a chronicle of leaving the first faiths to get to the deeper levels. Of stripping away the early experiences of faith to find if there was anything true there in the first place. It marks the trail of a journey—a journey through one "winter season" of my life, during which I learned about the silent-moving, life-bringing strength of true faith.

Chapter One
The Inner Room

A COLD NOVEMBER WIND slams against my New England house as I finish a phone conversation and hang up the receiver. Nine dead leaves still cling to the bare tree, visible through the window opposite me. Nine brown skeletons tenaciously holding on to what once gave them life— and now has gone cold and dry.

Six years ago I left California for this. Six years ago I left the warm climate, the warm fellowship, and what was the womb of my Christian life, and dragged my family kicking and screaming to this northern land of stark contrasts and these nine ghostly leaves.

For some time now, my reasons for doing this have escaped me. The impulse, the call, the motivation preceded any reasonable explanation. I still go into a stutter-start when someone asks me why I moved. There are no simple answers—at least none of the usual ones: no job back east, no relatives, no new ministry opportunities. It was more an inner push to leave there than a drawing to come here. My spiritual activities had dried up, and yet they continued to hang there, like leaves on a tree, no longer connected to the life I'd once felt coursing within me. Best to let the wind have them.

I've been here in New England long enough now to remember the maple outside in full leaf. Leaves as wide as the span of my hand fill its branches in the summer, making them sway and dance on the gentle breezes. Its trunk is strong, immoveable. With such rooted sturdiness, the branches can tease the wind—bending with it, dodging, then throwing it back into the face of the sky. On summer days, the whole tree smiles and spreads itself out in the sun, saturated with warmth, allowing the steady surge of chlorophyll to green the tips of its tiniest leaf-veins.

I can remember, in the same way, how the undeniable power of God made itself evident among our group of California believers twenty years ago, taking visible faith further than I had ever seen it go—out into veins of everyday real life. It was the early 1970s; it was the Jesus Movement; and I was caught up in its sweeping motion. I remember hearing the Scriptures taught in a way that finally made sense, and wondering why I'd never seen it so clearly before. I remember teaching Scripture—opening my mouth and not knowing exactly what to say and finding myself as amazed as the listener at what came out. I remember being a part of a team that was at the center of spiritual leadership and walking with a confidence that came from experiencing my childhood faith as it fleshed itself out for the first time in the concrete, light-of-day world. I can remember traveling with these teams to speak in other churches, seeing myself as part of a swashbuckling ministry, riding in and out of town with boots and Bible, like a spiritual "Butch Cassidy and the Sundance Kid" gang, leaving behind a cloud of dust and an amazed, enlightened crowd of townspeople wondering who those guys were, anyway.

These were my pre-marriage, pre-family, pre-credit card days. Foxes have holes, birds have nests, but the Son of Man and John Fischer had no place to lay their heads. No matter, I was free. I was operating without any encumbrances. The *New Testament* and my life had a primary relationship—indeed, I was living out its sacred pages, a sort of Acts 29 and beyond. This had to be it: the center of spiritual reality. If it wasn't, it was certainly the closest I was ever going to get.

The three most spiritual men I had ever been around had taken me under their wing. All at once I was in the same study with modern-day patriarchs. *Greek New Testaments* lay open on their laps, as the other student and I made notes in our *New American Standard Bibles* with KOO-I-NOOR pens, shaking them occasionally to keep the ink near the tip. With this pen, you could bold-face words without having to mess up your Bible with underlines. We would later joke that such pen shaking was a sign of true spirituality.

Joking was appropriate among these men; they were not spiritual at the expense of honesty. They joked so they wouldn't take each other so seriously. They joked so we wouldn't take them so seriously. They joked because they knew they could not take responsibility for the spiritual awakening we were all experiencing—only take advantage of it. They joked to maintain their humanity. Most of all—though I never realized it at the time—they joked to keep this sacred atmosphere, and our positions as leaders, from becoming an idol.

I was, unfortunately, too fond of standing next to the idol to get the joke. I laughed with them—but for other reasons. I laughed because it was so exhilarating to be in this Inner Room with such spiritual leaders that sometimes the air seemed thin. I laughed because I could hardly believe that I was *there*, with *them*—hearing from God, hearing truth meet reality, watching, before my very eyes, a sort of transfiguration of mortal men. It was the closest I would ever be to Jesus, Moses and Elijah in the flesh, and my response was similar to Peter's: "It is good for us to be here. Let us put up three tabernacles—one for Ray, one for Ron, and one for David." I didn't realize we were in the midst of a rare spiritual movement—on a mountaintop, from which we would one day have to descend.

And so, whatever else was happening in the world at

the time, it wasn't as significant as what was happening to me in that humble little study next to the church office: the study that was for me the inner circle—the mercy seat, as it were—of contemporary faith and the place where I took down all the answers to life's questions. I was there in the midst, at the center of everything. Men and women would always be this eager to hear the truth; truth would always be this easy to find; and finding would always be this rewarding.

Yes, the Jesus Movement really happened. I was a part of it. It wasn't just a fad or a social phenomenon triggered by a generation's disillusionment with the unclaimed dreams of the '60s, though these elements did play a part: It was a genuine movement of the Holy Spirit of God. For someone like me, who had grown up paying lip service to the credos of the faith, seeing the evidence of faith in front of me, in living color, was confirmation of what I already believed—and it was exhilarating! A high school Bible study group grew from thirty to 300 in a matter of weeks. High school kids were eager to open their Bibles and learn. On campuses, students began exhibiting all of the spiritual gifts, evangelizing their campus during lunch period and teaching the new believers during study hall, and high school ministry amounted to mostly "directing spiritual traffic." Large numbers of people were baptized on beaches and other public places, attracting passers-by, who became on-the-spot converts, moved by the testimonies of dripping wet believers.

This was the time in my life when a checking account was a compromise with unrighteous mammon, when insurance was lack of faith in God or lack of trust in the body of Christ, when a plan was dangerous because it might wipe out the spontaneous unpredictable wave of the Holy Spirit. This was the time when I would stay as a guest in someone's home and leave behind a note, saying, "Whatever town or village you enter, search for some worthy person there and stay at his house until you leave. As you enter the home, give it your greeting. If the home is deserving, let your peace rest on it; if it is not, let your peace return to you" (Matthew 10:11–13). To which I would add, "To a worthy home, I leave my greeting of peace," (my version of Acts 29:somewhere). I left behind many of these notes on the dining room tables of several believers across California in the 1970s, when branches were green and full and waving in the warm summer sun. . . .

Today, twenty years later, I think back on that pastors' study, where we bold-faced the truth in our Bibles, and it seems like a distant dream. The telescope of my memory looks back through the wide end and sees tiny figures in a small space where the truth is focused and precise as the tip of a black ink pen. As I do this, however, I realize this pen point now exists only in my mind. I am miles and years away from that room; and so are the men who were with me, who I looked up to so much at the time. If we could all return there—if indeed that room still exists—we would find it would never be the same, for now we all live out where truth is hidden and harder to pin down, among the brush strokes of our daily lives.

I stare out my window once again at the bony branches of the tree, now stripped of their lush greenery by the chill of autumn nights and the stiffening winds of the oncoming winter. I am suddenly aware that the branches of a tree behave differently in the wind when they are bare. There's no sway in them at all; they only rock stiffly in the cold air.

I chose to do this; for some time I've had to remind myself of that fact. I moved my family away. I came here to New England—to where trees lose their green leaf to heartless winter wind. I had to find out what would stand without the evangelical props that had always been present in my life. Was it truly my own faith I was living by—or was it someone else's? Was it the rewards and punishments of a group-sanctioned authority structure that kept me going? What was the life-sap of my faith? How would I find out? Who am I outside of the contexts that have so powerfully shaped my life thus far? What are my gifts and what is my own message? These questions were stirring in me unformed, at a level just below the surface back then, when I first chose to come here. I only knew I had to leave. You can't imagine what life would be without something, when that something is right in front of you, all around you, defining you.

It had always been right in front of me. For twelve years I was intimately involved with one of the most influential churches of the '70s. Four years prior to that, I attended one of the premier Christian colleges in the nation; before that, I spent my childhood through high school years immersed both socially and spiritually in another leading evangelical church.

I grew up with this faith. As a child, I was as much a part of it as it was a part of me. I wonder now how anyone could have matched the spiritual level of those surroundings with anything consistently real inside. Yes, I had a faith. I had a knowledge of God and what He had done for me that was real, but it was untested, unchallenged, untried by the realities of life that growing up demands. My faith was a part of me, but it was also a part of everything around me, and I don't think I was very good at distinguishing between the two. When faith is all connected up to your childhood identity—your sense of reward and punishment, your standing in society, your own place in the world—it's hard to reach into that switchboard of interconnected relationships and come up with a line that is truly your personal possession, a faith you would hold on to if all the rest were taken away. And even if you did have ahold of it, it would be hard to know for sure—and hard to tell it from everything else.

I also wonder about the growing up part. Growing up in any society ought to involve a definite point where an individual takes on certain responsibilities: you accept personal claims upon your relationships, your future, and your place in that society. I've often read how in certain Indian tribes, young braves go through physical ordeals to prove their manhood—feats of war or physical pain, or difficult treks into the wilderness, from which they return a man—this is their rite of passage, rich with a sense of ownership and destiny. Somehow I feel like I missed that ceremony. I long for an equivalent experience from which I could emerge suitably prepared to take on adult life.

Sometimes, too, I wonder if the Jesus Movement delayed my growth. Not that I question its validity, only its timing in relationship to my own growth process and my place in history. The other men in that inner circle, ten and twenty years my seniors, knew the Jesus Movement was just that—a movement, a passing spiritual season. In the wisdom of their experience, they knew that winter would follow this harvest of summer souls. I, on the other hand, was caught in the winds of that powerful spiritual summer—swept up and carried by them. My California faith was unprepared for the turnings of the seasons. I was young, impressionable, and a part of a highly idealistic generation that had tried unsuccessfully to create a new world where love and peace and meaning would prevail. The Jesus Movement, because it fulfilled many of these spiritual longings, also prolonged the myth of the new world that we had hoped for.

Six New England winters have caused me now to wonder: Did the Jesus Movement postpone, for some, the disillusionment of the '70s for another decade? For most of western society, the '70s were a time devoid of its own identity—a time to pack up the dreams of the '60s and return to the hated establishment. Protest songs became disco music and SDS leaders turned entrepreneurs. For Christians, on the other hand, the '70s brought the birth of a new sub-culture. While my pagan counterparts were shrink-wrapping their high ideals in the materialism that would eventually dominate the '80s, we born-again Christians were giving the old dream new life under a new banner. Though the spiritual realities of knowing Christ were real and lasting, I wonder if we used them to keep alive other ideologies that God never intended to perpetuate: we would remake the world with Christian politics; Christian economics; Christian T.V. , music. . . . I can remember thinking the world would never be the same because of what born-again Christians would achieve in my lifetime. I remember actually thinking I was going to be exempt from responsibilities in the real world, since we would always have our own world where the wind would always be warm and the leaves would always be green. . . .

And now twenty years and two mortgages later, I wake from what seems to be a deep sleep and look at the picture on my wall of my two closest buddies bringing me up out of the water in baptism—a picture that I once thought of as my only necessary credential for ministry, along with the fact that I was an intern at Peninsula Bible Church in California from 1970 to 1982. And I realize that picture means nothing in the real world, just as Peninsula Bible Church means nothing outside of the relatively few people that have been touched by it in relation to the rest of the world I travel in. I could perform weddings for the body of Christ in California because I had a license to ministry from Peninsula Bible Church; I had no idea that seventeen years later my piece of paper would be no more significant than a mail-order Universal Life Church ordination. ("You can get a license for anything in California," they sarcastically tell me here in Massachusetts.) In California, in 1972, they taught us, quoting Paul, that the only true credentials we would need would be the lives we would touch—and that is true in a spiritual sense. But the world does not operate in a spiritual sense. Slowly it has dawned on me that I have basked in a spiritual sun for ten years without any papers to show for it—nothing that can translate the personal rewards of those early days into a job, a career, an acceptable position in the world I live in now, twenty years later.

By 1980, the disillusionment that so many "secular" people had felt a decade earlier had finally begun to creep into my Christian consciousness. This wasn't Acts 29; it wasn't 70 A.D. It was *1,980* A.D. and the world was a different place. I had a wife and family responsibilities to take care of, and God was not going to do that for me.

Though I had access to individuals on the inside, I was no longer a part of the inner circle. Like the first cold wind of September that sends a shiver up the spine of a tree, I realized this euphoria was not going to last.

It had to be this way: The church—and each of us, its members—must go on regardless of the seasons (and it will live on or the tree would have died by now), but the spirit of the age blew on by and the next cold wind left me shuddering. I checked my history, my credentials and my bank book and found them all wanting—wanting for something real. Something substantial. Something I could call my own that I didn't even understand yet. I sought my own rite of passage, my own adult world, my own choices, and my own pain. I sought a place in a community that could not comfortably, instantly, easily recognize me by family, background or born-again faith.

I picked up and left for a place where no one was waiting for me to arrive—no one meeting the Christian musician stepping off the plane, no expectations. Just an as-yet unformed relationship with my own God and my own wife and my own two children. From all four I felt too detached, like dead leaves clinging to a tree in November.

And so six summers ago, I forced all of my family's earthly belongings into a 24-foot U-Haul truck and I-hauled it 3,000 miles from San Francisco to Boston, to this little town of Newbury, Massachusetts. No big church here; no discipleship program; no team ministry; no Christian community that we knew of; just a neighborhood, and a house with a wind-stripped maple tree visible out the window of my study.

Chapter Two
Leaving

THE SPENT LEAVES of the maple tree lie on the ground matted and brown . . . all but nine, that is. The loose upper layer of this carpet of leaves shrivels and curls—throwing back in my eye dabs of speckled light like the stubby strokes of a Monet masterpiece. What memories are these that lie scattered here? Memories of soft summer rains and warm nights under the stars; children laughing beneath the green-cool umbrella; birds singing and tenderly raising their young; squirrels chattering and scampering through the highways of branches?

With what protest did these leaves fall? Did they perform their seasonal descent with ease? Did they break from their hold and float to their matted grave, or did they hold on until the bitter end? Did they part from on high answering a call to fulfill nature's destiny, or were they released against their will? Who can say? It is said that "Parting is such sweet sorrow," and so it is. "Sorrow," because leaving signals the end of an era, a time cherished that can no longer be. But "sweet," because it puts you on the threshold of something new—something that cannot be unless the past is left behind.

I look out my window in early winter, and the best of the summer lies encapsulated in the slowly decomposing carpet at the foot of this tree; the future lies hidden within its bare branches. Life is drawn within . . . waiting . . . longing . . . sure that its time will come. Follow the leaf and the story ends; follow the tree, and it has only begun. . . .

He and I were standing on our redwood deck in El Granada, California when I first told him we were leaving. He had been my spiritual mentor throughout the years of my Christian training and early ministry. He had been the one who had ushered me into the inner room.

Standing there, silently staring at the distant twice-broken horizon of Pacific ocean that you could see from our deck, I recalled a dinner he and I had shared not long before with the senior pastor/teacher of our fellowship, who we fondly called "Umgawa"—a term we borrowed from California surf-lore . . . "Umgawa" was the fictitious god of The Big Wave. We called him this because we truly meant to marvel—not only at his prophetic gift, but at his ability to take a joke.

At the time, the three of us had been on a ministry team to a Christian college, and had stolen away for a late-evening meal—far away from the dining hall, the students, and the demands of the ministry, to a restaurant on the top of the space needle in Seattle. Since it was Umgawa's sixty-third birthday, the conversation had taken on the flavor of a life-in-review, inspiring both of these men to comment on how close they were to the finish line, how ready they were to go, how much they felt that they had accomplished with their lives so far, and what was left to be done.

This conversation only served to heighten the sense of disillusionment I felt as the Jesus Movement slowed down. These guys were on their way *out* and I was still on my way *in* to—what? I realized I didn't know. What were they leaving behind for me? Did they care? If they felt at all the autumn wind that was threatening to strip my soul bare, it was only signaling to them the golden years of their lives and ministries. To me it was the harbinger of a long cold winter. Like a young sapling, privileged to grow under the protection of greater trees, I felt cold in the shadows that their personalities cast across the table. I felt the tenderness of my branches and the fragility of my new growth in their stalwart presence. "Let no one despise your youth," Paul says to Timothy. All well and good, but you cannot fake years of experience. And I, there in the shadows at the top of the space needle in Seattle, was most definitely lacking experience as I realized that my secure position was coming to an end. Without these men, who was I?

In the wise words I heard that night, as we slowly revolved above the Seattle skyline, I understood the value of experience. I heard a maturity that comes not necessarily from being smart, but from the mere fact that you have years and seasons under your belt, however well you've lived them. The 63-year-old drunk on the street speaks from the same school: the school of hard knocks; the school of life. That night, I felt only the glib leanness of my years, and I knew I needed to enroll in that school regardless of the rising cost of tuition. . . .

As my mentor and I stood a few feet apart on my deck, not looking at each other, but out toward the horizon I felt the long shadow of his experience again. There was security there, a presence much bigger than life. I was still proud of him, proud to have known him and to have been graced by his life. Yet I knew that if I stayed in this protecting shade I would become too comfortable. I did not resent the shade, I only feared my desire to stay under it. I knew myself too well.

There is a part of me forever content to stay in the shadows. Shadows are defined. They make a line on the ground. You either stay in them or step out of them. It's easier to be defined by someone else's shadow than to stand in your own sun. Taking your own sun means you have to make your own choices. You have to step out and risk and bear the consequences. But there was this other part of me that I could not shut up—the part that was not content to be defined by the lines cast by someone else's shadow: I wanted to be out where I could cast my own.

For some reason, as we stared at the ocean I thought about John and Charles Wesley: how John would preach and Charles would write a song on the spot and teach it to the people. That was what I could do. I could be a Charles Wesley to all these great John Wesleys around me—put their teachings to music. I loved teaching and the clearly defined precepts of the Word. But something in me resisted this well-defined role—some undefined person was stirring within that the *teacher* in me didn't understand. Something told me I must find my own content, my own voice; I must stand in my own sun. I might have thought differently about leaving, had I known then that this same sun could get as cold as it does in New England, and that regardless of its shining, the cold air could strip a tree so bare that the only shadow it makes is a slight etching on the ground—not even enough for someone to stand in.

However, on my deck in the shadow of a fuller tree, looking out at the Pacific, unaware of frozen sunshine, I knew what I had to do. I was to go as far east as I could drive, where the shadows are the longest and the sun is the coldest.

It was not a good parting. He referred to debts I had incurred, which the equity in my house would clear up. That was the only reason for my leaving we could talk about, though we both knew there were other reasons and they were more important. How could we talk about what I only barely understood myself? How could I speculate about his shadow and its effect on me while I stood there under the weight and breadth of it?

Leaving is always hard.

Babies part from the womb. From its glowing warm-red envelopment, from the constant swishing of its mother's heart-blood, from the cord of life that fed it continuously, effortlessly, a baby is wrenched out of its human cocoon—out to where it must scream for air, scream for food, scream to be touched, scream to be made warm again, scream for room to grow. There are paths through lifetime relationships and beyond, and it's necessary to follow those paths for life to move on, and it is always uncomfortable in the passing. The long progression is begun; one day a man parts from his parents.

We want to move on, most of us, to leave the securities that will no longer satisfy our growing longings. But we fear, as well—fear the cold reality of living without them.

The nine leaves outside my window have hung on through the first terrible winter winds. What makes them hold? The leaves are already dead. Is it the tree that refuses to let them go, the way parents hang on to the memory of their son as a boy and refuse to see the man?

There are more wombs in our life after we leave our mothers'. Anything can be a womb: we can depend too much upon any environment that provides protection and soft walls around us. Our mothers' bodies were rude to us: they forced us out with little warning. Should we find ourselves in another womb later in life, we are the ones who are left to do the pushing. And if we would grow—follow the path to someplace new, higher, better—we will have to become more heartless with ourselves.

A scene flashes across my mind today as I rake the leaves outside. An odd scene, coming up, I suppose, from the depths of my soul since it's not a memory. A melancholy scene. There are lots of leaves to rake, and they aren't going anywhere. I lean on my rake and let the scene roll before my eyes, hoping to learn what my soul is trying to tell me. . . .

The father stands white-faced, like an ivory statue, with

pursed lips, staring at the railway platform. The hat and overcoat dwarf his large frame, his shoulders bearing the weight of all those silent years. Next to him, the son is half-hearing his mother's voice. She is speaking, too often and too long, stories and sermons about his failings, which he has heard many times over. He feels as if all these words are crushing the love he knows they all three long to hold. Her husband does nothing to stop her; he has never understood why these moments always bring such a heavy weight to bear upon him. He gave up wondering long ago, and settled into controlled impatience, an ache to have this uncomfortable wall of words behind them. His ears—far keener to the whistle of the train and the conductor's call than the ill-timed voice of his wife—recognize the imminent way of escape. Now they hurry their son onto the train, fumbling with tickets, last-second fears, and last-second love with which she tries in vain to cover the fresh wounds her words have cut into the young man's heart.

The son watches as his parents grow smaller on the receding platform. *Why now?* he muses, his face frozen in the window. *Why not yesterday when this could have been discussed? Why does she always have to have the last word?* And why was his father so silent? Somewhere in that departing train and its destination are reasons for his leaving that his parents would probably never understand. But he knows he must leave if he ever hopes to overcome the same weaknesses buried in his own character.

He watches them standing huddled on the platform—waving, becoming smaller and smaller. They will stay, their courses largely determined already by their own choices (or lack of them). His whole life lies before him.

He knows, even feels their love—but why is there always this painful after-shock? Why does he feel he is throwing off chains the farther the train pulls away from the station? And what kind of strange love is this—known more in absence than in communion? Something about their pressure suffocates his own sense of loving and of being loved until, in moments such as these, when his parents recede, he feels the strangle-grip loosen. The love breathes once again; but along with it comes the aching sense of disappointment that love between them could not be known and experienced when they are together. He fears it will never be, and he tries to push out thoughts of their inevitable passing when he will stare at their lifeless forms and know the final disappointment. He knows the love is there, but all he gets are last-second words. What will he say then, when he has the last word? He feels his mouth dry and half-open, looking for a word as the train speeds away. . . .

Leaving is a part of God's design for growth, but He never said it would be easy. I continue my raking, musing now about what it must have been like for Jesus to leave His parents.

Once when Jesus was speaking to a crowd, someone told Him, "Your mother and brothers are standing outside, wanting to speak to you." I envision them waiting impatiently for Jesus. What is it they want? Theirs is a special relationship, perhaps they want some kind of privileged treatment—an introduction, an honored seat in the crowd, perhaps just a little bit of His time right now, when He would choose them over everyone else, making them feel important.

Why were His mother and brothers out *there* in the first place? Why weren't they in the crowd viewing with equal amazement His authority, the effect of His words on people, and His mysterious healing touch? Maybe because they weren't amazed. They knew who this was; they grew up with this boy. *He's the son of a carpenter like the rest of us.* For this reason Jesus could not perform many miracles in His home town. He had to leave.

So when they asked Him what to do about His mother and brothers, He replied, "Who is my mother, and who are my brothers?" Pointing to the disciples and the crowd, He said, "Here are my mother and my brothers. For whoever does the will of my Father in heaven is my brother and sister and mother."

Such a statement must have endeared Him to the crowd—and put a knife in His family members. What was it they wanted? Maybe they had some other agenda going on, and that's why they needed this private conversation "outside" the crowd. "Jesus, we just wanted to let you know we're having a little family get-together tomorrow night at James' place. We'd really be disappointed if you didn't make it. You know it's his birthday and all, and . . . well . . . he thinks the world of you. Can we look forward to seeing you there? Shall we put you down for a guest? (We were hoping you wouldn't bring all twelve of these guys. . . .)"

Or . . . "Jesus, I have some of your things here that you left behind: your letterman's jacket from Nazareth High, hiking boots—(you could sure use those now)—and your Sony Walkman. I also baked some of your favorite cookies. You know, your father hasn't seen you in some time. He was asking about you just the other day."

Mary should have known better. She was there when He was twelve years old and they left Him behind in Jerusalem, and after frantically searching for Him for three days at the gym, the video arcade, the local Pizza Hut and in the parking lot of McDonald's where pre-adolescents hang out on Saturday nights to watch the older kids drag, they finally found Him in the synagogue, the last place they would have looked and the first place they should have, sitting among the teachers listening to them and asking them questions. "Son, why have you treated us like this? Your father and I have been anxiously searching for you all over town." And she had heard the reply that must have cut at her heart painfully, dividing it between her human desire as a mother and her holy desire as a woman of God: "Why were you searching for me all over town? Didn't you know I had to be in my Father's house?" The boy had already left: He had left His earthly father to get on board another train and do His real Father's business.

Now His relatives are standing on the platform trying to pull Him back, but He is already on-board with a new family, one that is far bigger than His mother and brothers were able to see at the time.

Leaving is always hard.

But like the child in the womb and the son boarding the train, and like me heading toward the eastern sun, something bigger than Nazareth was pulling on the robe of Jesus. It happens to all of us—or at least it should. We sense that we are growing out of the forms that mold us and that our lives want to take on their own shape. In order to constantly experience growth, we have only to let it happen. There will always be a pushing against the walls of smallness in the life of a Christian—leaving womb for world, father for Father, self for God, even earthly life for the eternal expanse of heaven. To restrict, to restrain, to narrow one's view is to work against the will of God. Mary had her eyes for a moment on herself and her sons; Jesus had His eyes on His Father, the world and eternity.

Is this not the way we first came to know Him? We moved out of the small choking confines of self and sin— the denials and rationalizations that had become our comfort—and taking a step of faith, we let go of the small hungry hands of our addictions to reach for the big hand of God. But having reached for Him, do we have Him? Did I get it? Did I grab hold of the hand of God? Am I holding on tight? Do I have it now?

I wonder. Why do I feel as if I'm still reaching? Is it because, like Jacob, though I may wrestle with God, I can never fully have Him within my grasp (a heel or a foot, maybe, and only for a moment. . .)?

Always reaching but never fully grasping. Like the Apostle Paul who says he is always pressing on "to take hold of that for which Christ Jesus took hold of me," we press on, as well. The implication is: though God has a hold of me, I do not, cannot, fully have ahold of Him. Why is this? *Because His hand is so much bigger than mine?*

This is the tension and the frustration that keeps me reaching and growing. It's a good tension, though no less frustrating. It produces good results because it forces me out of the confines of the comfortable.

Because His hand is so much bigger than mine. . . . Though He has me, I don't fully have Him. It sounds unfair, but He chooses to have it this way. He wants my participation. It's what keeps me grabbing. It's the "grab-back" of faith. *I want* "to take hold of that for which Christ Jesus took hold of me . . ." It's amazing to think that Paul is still saying this near the end of his life; proof that he doesn't have it yet.

Paul kept grabbing; I keep grabbing. God has hold of me; I am still reaching, grabbing for Him.

Because His hand is so much bigger than mine. . . . If I have ahold of something small enough for human hands to hold on to, chances are it isn't God, or very little of Him.

. . . probably only a few dead leaves I'm refusing to release to this winter wind.

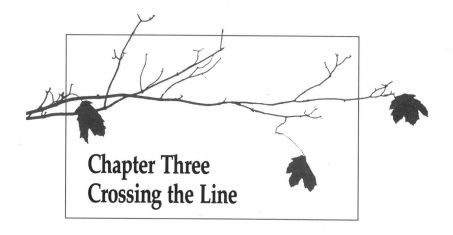

Chapter Three
Crossing the Line

IT NEVER CEASES to amaze me, the incredible network of roadways that connect this country. That I can pull out of a driveway in San Francisco and into one in Newbury, Massachusetts with the same ease as I would go across town to see a friend, with five days being the only difference, is remarkable.

It was during this drive that I crossed the "line" I had been sensing inside, though I never knew what to call it.

There is what I call an imaginary line, reaching back to the medieval period and stretching through the Reformation, the Enlightenment, the discovery of the New World, the early American revivals, and right on into the contemporary Christian culture of today: it is the line that separates the sacred from the secular, church from the world, Christians from non-Christians, and "us" from "them."

Even though Jesus, friend of sinners, incarnation of God, disregarded this line by passing freely on either side of it, it seems we Christians refuse to be convinced, for we like the way it orders our world. We like the way this line allows us to control our spirituality and confirm our guilt. We like the way it enables us to arrange the people, places and ideas of our confusing existence into compartments that no longer require our thinking and evaluation. We like the way this line simplifies our lives. We use the line as a means of choosing up sides. We have no intention of leaving the *comforts* of the secular, we simply use the line to mean that when we are on the secular side, dealing with things of the world, we do not have to concern ourselves with spiritual things. Spiritual things are over there, we are over here, for the time being, and we pass like chameleons from side to side. In this double-minded behavior, we are much more like the Gnostics of long ago, who felt that if you believed the right things you could live any way you pleased. What you did in the physical realm was irrelevant to your spiritual beliefs.

It is true that we must learn to live in both realms. Christian ascetics—those of the past and the present—are wrong to think they can become so spiritual that real everyday needs and obligations will all be "covered" by God in the way, for instance, that God sent ravens to feed Elijah when he was hungry. But gnostics, including many Christians today, are wrong to think that they can coexist in two realms that are contradictory to each other *without seeking to resolve the dilemma*. The answer, as Jesus showed us, is to live in both realms, but have one mind—to live with the sacred so present in you, wherever you are, that the line is no longer necessary. Or, to say it in a different way, it is to live with such simple confidence in God and His love and acceptance that you stop brow-beating yourself and everyone else with spiritual standards; it is to care about people more than yourself and your own need to be right; it is to trust God for others.

All this comes down to having your spiritual eyes opened. Two people can look at the same thing and see it entirely differently. The Pharisees saw Jesus at Levi's party and saw Him partaking with sinners. Jesus, at the same time, was more aware of the sacred worth of these "sinners," of these men and women whom He had created in His own image and for whom He would soon die. The

Pharisees, always aware of the line, saw only compartments. Jesus saw the line melt away into human faces.

I first crossed the line somewhere in the state of Nebraska on Interstate 80 in a 24-foot U-Haul truck with "ADVENTURE IN MOVING" written on back and with all our belongings inside and car in tow. I could have sent all the stuff in a moving van and flown to Boston. At the time, I used the excuse that I was trying to save money, but as it turned out, the cost was not that much different. The real reason was that I wanted to do this. There was something important about personally transporting all our belongings across the country. Something about packing in everything at one door and driving it up to the other and getting to know every inch of the pavement in between.

I see it now as my own way of going out from all that was sacred, of crossing the line, carrying my personal belongings and my family with me. An airplane trip would have lifted me up out of the one and deposited me into the other in a fraction of the time, with little or no connection between the two, like the gnostic nature of a suspended flight. I wouldn't have known the great distance I was covering. How would I be sure that the faith I brought across the line was my own if I didn't carry it across myself?

This move was the reverse of the pioneers. I was conscious of this many times as I followed the rhythmic disappearance of the broken white line under the left side of the truck's hood. It was the reverse of the average Christian life, as well. I was going back to a "before," a time corresponding to the pre-Christian days of most believers, when their relationships were predominantly non-Christian and their world was largely secular.

I knew enough about my destination to know it was going to represent the other side of the line for me. For the first time in my life, I was not moving to a church, a fellowship, or a Christian institution. There was nothing prearranged and no one waiting for us to arrive, just an empty house and a new neighborhood. And I knew that our intention was to take up our place in that neighborhood—to make community a priority over church, and non-Christian a priority over Christian.

I wanted to lose the line forever—and to find out if, in the deepest recesses of my heart, there was any real faith to guide and shape my life and the way I thought about and treated other people. I wanted to find out if that faith could survive the darkest, coldest winter. I wanted to know the questions to all my answers; the despair that stands opposite my hope; the lostness next to finding; the sin that required the death of the Son of God; the "befores" of my well-rehearsed "afters"; the winter of the summer of my faith. Not that I might never know again the green leaves of summer, but that I might know, in a deeper way, the sap to which they owe their life. That I might know God apart from my circumstances—whether my life is working or it is not. That I might simply know Him.

I drove with a friend, a companion from California, who accompanied me on this trans-continental journey and later flew back to San Francisco. Marti and the children flew to Florida to stay with her mother, while I went ahead to move us in.

The truck made it across country and past the last toll-booth on the Masspike—and then gave out on Route 128, forty-five minutes from the front door of our soon-to-be new house. So we left it there, unhitched the car from the tow-bar and drove the last thirty miles unencumbered—like walking in street shoes after wearing heavy roller skates for a couple hours. I'll never forget the feeling rounding the final corner at the edge of Newbury's Upper Green, where you can see the house for the first time. We had previously seen 24 Green Street for all of fifteen minutes, and had made our final decision to buy from back on the west coast. Now I was shaking with an overdose of excitement and fear as I faced, for the first time, the physical consequences of my decision to move. Everything inside of me felt stretched out like a rubber band—a very thin rubber band close to snapping. I almost stumbled over my weightless feet as I approached the door.

The next day I closed the deal in a lawyer's office in Boston. My friend and I celebrated over lunch in an outdoor cafe on Tremont Street before he flew back to California—leaving me totally alone in an empty house, a long, long way from all things familiar. . . .

Six years now have come and gone since that first afternoon here all alone. I'm looking out my window right now at what remains of another summer, still hanging on a tree.

I knew there was going to be more to it. The line we crossed in Nebraska wasn't the half of it. By moving away from my secure, defined, Christian environment, and enduring cold, like the maple tree outside my window, I began to discover information about myself and about life that I needed to find—for myself and for others like me. You could say that I needed to find my true colors.

Now most of us know, as regarding a tree and its leaves, that the many shades of green we see in spring and summer are caused by the presence of a green pigment named chlorophyll. All those green leaves out there possess other colors, too, but these are cloaked by the chlorophyll. You could say the leaves are green, but you could also say the leaves are red, orange, yellow or purple; and in the shorter cooler days of autumn, the chlorophyll breaks down, revealing the other pigments, the hidden colors of the leaves that were there all along.

It could be argued that it makes no difference what season I am in, or what deeper selfishnesses still lie buried within me, as long as I am covered by the "chlorophyll" of the Spirit. If I walk in the Spirit, I will simply be, and stay, green. It sounds like a reasonable argument. Yet I have seen in myself, and in others, a tendency to hide the true colors of our flesh behind a supposed greenness, so we never have to see what we are truly like: If someone notices a flaw, we are too quick to hide behind the bumper-sticker-thin wall, "Well, I'm not perfect, just forgiven"; or to hide behind sanitized Christian activities, like church attendance or Bible studies.

Why would Paul have taken such pains to specify the works of the flesh in as much detail as the works of the Spirit, unless he wanted us to be able to recognize and deal with them? Like the leaves of a tree, "dying to self" means first recognizing the pigments of self that are my particular propensity, the lies I must be most conscious of, if I'm going to strip them away and see myself as I really am.

Contrary to much popular Christian teaching, sin is hardly ever the real problem for the believer. We do the body of Christ a huge disservice when we make sin the big issue. What is the most commonly taught alternative to sin? Simple: *Stop sinning!* Oh great. That's a big help. Let's all go out there and stop sinning! Okay you guys, read my lips, "No more sinning!" This kind of thinking always ends up in the same place: more sinning and more covering it up.

The issue for me as a believer is not sin, it's *denial*. Saying and acting as if you don't have sin is a Christian's biggest downfall.

"If we claim to be without sin, we deceive ourselves and the truth is not in us" (1 John 1:8). John saw it coming. He made sure we had a way of seeing through this lie. This lie is the gnosticism of living on both sides of the line without conflict. "If we claim we have not sinned, we make him out to be a liar and his word has no place in our lives" (1 John 1:10). These are fairly harsh words and, surprisingly enough, they are not aimed at sinners but at those who try to pass themselves off as sinless saints.

Gingerly sandwiched in between these two warnings about self-righteousness is the verse most Christians know the best out of this chapter: "If [on the contrary instead of hiding it and lying about it] we confess our sins, he is faithful and just and will forgive us our sins and purify us from all unrighteousness" (1 John 1:9). *If we confess. . . .* That means, according to my Greek lexicon, *to speak the same, to agree (be of one mind).* In other words, if I see this thing as God sees it—"This is sin. This is ugly. I'm in deep trouble here"—then I will be forgiven. First I've got to see myself as I really am; then there is a way out.

This is the reason why my Christianity was in the abstract for so long. I believed. I really did believe, but I believed in a Son of God (whom I couldn't see) who died on a cross (that I couldn't see) for my sins (that I *wouldn't* see) so I could go to heaven (which I can't see). What sense did my beliefs make in my real life? Not much—until I crossed a line within, and started to recognize the only thing I am able to see. It is the doorway, as it were, into all the others: It is my sin. If I can see my sin, then I can begin to get a view of the cross, of Christ himself, and even a vision of heaven to come. Otherwise it's all a neat little formula, a nice booklet, a wonderful plan for someone else's life, or the Wordless Book that they used to take us through every week in Sunday School when I was a kid—the one with nothing but four colored pages: *Black* for my sin, *Red* for the blood of Jesus that washes my sin away until I am as *White* as snow, and *Gold* for the color of the streets I will walk on someday in heaven. Great story. True story. And, oh yes, there was something mentioned about disobeying your parents or beating up on your little sister—but the adults, who were responsible for teaching me from the Wordless Book, never said a word about their own *Black* page. After a long time of never hearing anything about anybody's *Black* page, I just assumed you didn't have to deal with that part anymore. We were all *White* now, waiting for streets of *Gold*. Why not skip that first part, then, and go right to the *White* page?

For a person trained to think like me, seeing my own sin and owning up to it has never been an easy thing. I have developed a most elaborate network of ways to insure myself of never having to encounter *my own sin* in all its awfulness—which is how God looks at it. If this is what confession means—*to be of one mind*—then I've got to agree with God that there are life-destroying, self-promoting lies in me and they are disgusting. Plus I have had the support of a model Christian family and a long history of denial, couched in faithful ministry, to bolster my inability to face these things.

I'll never forget what it was like to see my sin for the first time (and I'm not talking about masturbation, that most famous of private Christian sins, which we falsely believe to be our most ugly and secret vice, and never encounter the real ugliness of ourselves). I'm talking about the first time I saw myself, not through my own private eyes but through someone else's eyes—someone who saw my sin and had been deeply hurt by it. That's when I first became dimly aware that there was such a thing as real sin in my life, of which I could be totally blind.

It happened over a Christmas vacation, when a bunch of us were home from our second year in college, and watching our childhood friendships slip away. We were four high school buddies, trying to carry adolescent relationships into adult life. We probably should have let them go, since that's what eventually happened to them. At the time, however, we were tenacious and wanted to hold on. The result, though it didn't accomplish what we had hoped it would, did prove valuable at least to me—valuable, though painful. It was my first hard look at another pigment in my flesh, which was concealed from me by my "Christianity."

The whole thing began when someone suggested we stay up all night and talk. We'd gathered originally under the pretense of an evening of Rook ("Christian playing-cards," to some). At the close of an otherwise shallow evening, one guy spoke up: "Look, is this it? Are we going to get together once a year and play cards, while our lives grow further and further apart? We've all spent two years at different colleges, growing in different directions. All we still have together are childhood memories. What am I now? Who are you? What are we becoming? How will we ever know if we just get together once a year and play

Rook? If this is all our relationship has come to, then I, for one, am ready to hang it up."

Well said, we all thought—but what do we do about it? I'll never forget the next scene, for it was a monumental turning point in my life. We were standing on the porch of my parents' house late at night when this challenge was made. The next step was uncertain. Someone suggested what we needed was at least a whole night awake to really probe into each other's lives, a sort of marathon encounter group. We all felt a little bit frightened. Then someone said, "Why not tonight; right now?" Now we really *were* frightened because we all realized this was it. If we didn't do it now, we would never do it.

"Well," I said, sucking in my breath, "my parents are gone. We have the house to ourselves. Why not?" Nervously excited, we all returned inside, and settled in for what was to be twelve hours of non-stop group therapy.

One of the guys had had some experience with this through a psychology course. He had been the one with the "marathon" suggestion, so we looked to him for direction, and he came up with some rules we all agreed upon. A chair was designated as the "hot seat." When your name came up, you sat in the designated place and were not allowed to speak until the other three had thoroughly exhausted the subject at hand, which was *you.* Any defense, even clarification, was absolutely forbidden until your three friends were certain they'd said everything they had ever thought or felt about you. Then you had a chance to speak, and they were to keep silent until you were done. This was followed by a brief time of open forum—a kind of interaction with the whole process and what we were discovering. Then it was on to the next guy.

The sun came up on our inquisition. It was the first time I'd ever crossed the line, gotten outside myself, to see me as other people see me (apart from the polite things people say). The major ground-rule was that we had to be totally honest.

And so in the faint light of an early dawn I heard three

friends talking about me. I found out that I was an extremely selfish person; I used people for what they could do for me; I'd hurt all three of them—one very deeply; I was disloyal and had trampled on their loyalty; they were disgusted with my condescension and the fact that I could always run home and be found right regardless of how wrong I was. They all liked me, but they truly wondered if I cared, or was capable of caring for anyone other than myself and my own high-ranking spiritual reputation.

It was my first hard look at the true colors of my *self*, stripped of the "green" of my Christian head-trip. The first time I glimpsed my real sins of the flesh—my hiding behind spirituality, Christian heritage, spiritual reputation; my pride.

I learned from that experience that there is a better alternative to sin than denying, or covering it up—it's the way of honest confession. We cried and prayed and hugged each other and went home exhausted—and I don't know about them, but a door was left open in me so that I could never be the same.

God, I now know, continually rakes through the dead leaves of our characters. I keep wishing this will be finished someday . . . and still my earthly seasons keep their steady, relentless cycle. What are the pigments I hide behind today—the xanthophyll, carotene and anthocyanins that lurk in the veins of my flesh? Will it take another all-night encounter session to find them, or am I getting better at this? The Holy Spirit does a fine job of convicting us that something lies deeper than our fear or anger or denial, if we sit still and listen.

I'm listening more carefully now, a few New England frosts have showed me new things in this, my flesh; the cold has sucked away the green. . . .

For one thing, I have seen that I fear man more than I fear God. It saddens me to have trampled on His grace—yet it feels good to let the shorter days finally reveal a true color that has been hidden there for so long: Yes, I am more concerned about what people think of me than what God thinks.

I realized this recently while reading through letters to the editor concerning magazine articles I've written. I was arranging them in "favorable" and "non-favorable" piles, when I realized the unfavorable ones filled me with horror. I knew that, in person, my strong stands would fly out the window if I had to face one disgruntled reader: Were that person here in front of me, I would most likely smooth over what I once held to so passionately. I can't stand to have a person not think well of me. I would like to say it is always the truth I fight for, but I'm afraid my true colors often reveal only a purple pride: I must be liked at all times.

If someone came to my door who had the power to cause me to lose my reputation in the Christian community or to lose my wife and children, I would hesitate with this choice. I know, because I've come to see how I've sacrificed them at times in lesser ways. It's easy to get on a plane and be *somebody* to an unknown group of people. It's easy to exercise a large amount of faith for a short period of time and think I am doing great things for God—when all along I am carefully portioning out the smallest amounts of myself, and my faith, at home. Learning to be changed by my faith at home, to be consistent about this over the long haul, is the real work of faith required of me. So often I'm unwilling to attend to this.

How often do I think about the future in terms of my family's security, their dreams and goals, as well as my own? I'm satisfied with a future that assures me of my own comfort zone, but how much do I make them sacrifice so that I can stay comfortable?

I sometimes wonder if these regular trips have enabled me to continue some sort of single life free from the encumbrances Paul talks about in 1 Corinthians 7: "An unmarried man is concerned about the Lord's affairs—how he can please the Lord. But a married man is concerned about the affairs of this world—how he can please his wife—and his interests are divided."

For three weekends out of a month, when I travel to minister, I get to be an unmarried man and concern myself only with "things of the Lord." It almost sounds like it might be a good thing, but for me it is wrong. God would not be asking me to sacrifice my marriage for Him when it's out of the honesty of my marriage that I ought to minister. The conflict Paul refers to in this passage is the wrestling match of honesty a married person must face, not escape. Until I figure out how to bring my wife and children along with me in my heart and my mind, then I am not truly married—not all the time. I'm actually reluctant to call home sometimes when I'm on the road, because something might need my attention, and I don't wish to deal with the divided sense that would rise in my heart.

There have been other, not-so-subtle sacrifices, like the time I sacrificed my wife's integrity for a record deal. There was a season, before we moved to New England, when Marti was my business manager, at least up until the time when there was a conflict between her word and the word of the record company. Because I was afraid of losing the deal, I let her reputation go down without a fight. I didn't even see what I was doing at the time—or maybe I chose not to. In the summer-green contentment that I would get to minister on yet another album, I never saw hidden in me the color of yellow cowardice.

More colors revealed by dying: I fear facing the bill collector or the IRS man more than I fear facing the throne of God. I could cover this up by saying I am secure in His grace, but His grace makes a person able to trust Him and act. So often I fear the consequences of obeying God, and start stalling. Where is my fear of God? I have so many other fears before which I prefer to cower.

I know I have a deep and lasting love for God, but I am realizing now that I do not trust Him. I know very little of what it truly means to trust. I trust my bank account, and I trust more than God those who can fill that account or deplete it. Anyone who has more money than I do is bigger than me; some of them are bigger than God. I read the Psalmist, "In God I trust; I will not be afraid," and I know this is not me because I choose, rather, to be afraid. Peace in my life is more attached to the last figure in my check-book than to the presence of God. And should I suspect that figure will be inadequate to meet my needs, I choose not to even know it, but to shrink from it and hide my love and my living in the smallness of the fear of it all.

Oh God, it's so ugly. I had to get to this, didn't I?

Curse the tree outside my window. Curse that which would reveal such hurt and pain. Curse and bless. Curse and bless.

There are numerous ways of handling the leaves that fall from this tree in autumn the way old memories and old ways of thinking fall. I have lived in New England long enough to have tried them all. One approach is to let them all fall and then rake and bag everything in one major effort. The problem with this is that snow usually falls by the time the leaves are all down, and once that happens the chances of getting them bagged up before next spring are slim. The systematic approach, raking and bagging every week through the autumn months, is probably the most favorable, but I'm not disciplined enough to schedule this. So there always seems to be a layer of soggy leaves, sometimes still in flattened mounds, unbagged piles that have lain under snow all winter and have to be removed in March to allow for new grass coming up under the tree.

This is another color of my flesh there in the frozen piles of untended leaves: selective laziness. I am not generally lazy, but I will often busy myself with something trivial so I don't have to encounter the complex or the uncomfortable. I am lethargic when it comes to the most important.

For instance, in the first few weeks at our new house in Newbury, I was there alone working on repairs and preparing for the family's arrival. Marti and the children stayed in Florida because the bathroom had to be completely gutted, and it would be a major inconvenience. I had decided

49

it was best for them to stay there until I was done.

What started as a temporary separation turned into an indefinite amount of time, because I had to leave my work periodically for personal engagements on the road. Hindsight tells me it would have been better to keep the family together and bear the hardship. But the truth of the matter was, I liked being alone, having nothing to do but unimportant things that had suddenly become important. My paternal family is famous for this. My parents will come visit and we will immediately get to work busying ourselves with household projects—scraping, painting, pasting, hacking, needling. On and on it goes. My wife can't stand it. She takes the children with her and goes off and runs a Chamber of Commerce, or organizes a waterfront festival, or something of comparable importance. When she returns, we're still needling and hacking and stripping and washing down. That's when she puts a stop to all this and makes us sit down and have a conversation. (A what? A *conversation?* What will we say?) My wife is a sort of painful savior to my family. She can easily tackle the confronting job of my three high school buddies all by herself.

At one point during my preparation time here alone, I got involved with trying to salvage eighteen small New England-type latches that were on the cupboards in the kitchen. They'd been painted black and looked pretty ugly, until I applied paint remover and found out they were made of brass and pewter. I decided to restore them. Three days later they were done and I could look forward to proudly displaying the results of my niggling rescue operation. I was even thinking about writing an article about the hidden treasures I'd found and all the related spiritual implications. Which is all well and good, except that the real hidden treasures for me at the time were the lives of my wife and children waiting 1500 miles away to be rescued by their husband and father. I chose to rescue eighteen brass and pewter New England kitchen cupboard latches instead.

I know now that a certain pigment in my leaves would

prefer to be left alone without any attachments. I would prefer to *never* have to make a decision or encounter one major entanglement. I would love to indulge in an inactive mind. If God makes personal hells for people where they will spend their agonizing eternities in the way their ugly flesh wanted it all along, I have a feeling this would be mine: to be forever alone with an endless list of unimportant things to do.

Yes, the piles of leaves in my back yard are like fleeting monuments to a supposed spirituality. There never seems to be an end to this. No sooner do I get these gathered into piles than a fresh gust of autumn scatters them again. I would let them all go until next March—except I need to know what these leaves reveal about my self: I need, at last, to wake up to who I really am—my true colors.

The things I must stay "awake" to are so basic, but I forget them: first, that I am loved and forgiven; second, that I have a job to do commensurate with what I have been gifted to do. The job—which is mainly to love others more than myself—is not really hard once I begin. Like raking these leaves, it's only hard if I neglect it, if I only think or talk about doing it. Once I begin, the power is there. My part is to begin—which means throwing the weight of my conviction *and*, yes, real human effort into it. I've got to stay awake to that fact, to remember.

I looked up the word "remember" in my concordance this morning and found 350 references. Most of the time it's a directive, from God to us, to remember Him and the things He has taught us. He must have anticipated that some of us were going to have a problem with this. Here are a few of the most memorable. I think of them today as I look out at November leaves still blowing across the yard and a few dead ones (now it is only four) still clinging to the tree.

"*Remember* that my life is but a breath . . ." (Job 7:7).

"I *remembered* my songs in the night" (Psalm 77:6).

"However many years a man may live, let him enjoy them all. But let him *remember* the days of darkness, for

51

they will be many" (Ecclesiastes 11:8).

"You who have escaped the sword, leave and do not linger! *Remember* the Lord in a distant land . . ." (Jeremiah 51:50).

" . . . and don't you *remember*? When I broke the five loaves for the five thousand, how many basketfuls of pieces did you pick up?" (Mark 8:18, 19).

"I have told you this, so that when the time comes you will *remember* that I warned you" (John 16:4).

" . . . *Remember* that at that time you were separate from Christ" (Ephesians 2:12).

"*Remember* my chains" (Colossians 4:18).

"*Remember* those earlier days after you had received the light, when you stood your ground in a great contest in the face of suffering" (Hebrews 10:32).

"*Remember* the height from which you have fallen!" (Revelation 2:5).

"*Remember*, therefore, what you have received and heard; obey it, and repent. But if you do not wake up, I will come like a thief, and you will not know at what time I will come to you" (Revelation 3:3).

Remember. Remember. Rake and remember; stay awake. . . .

Remembering and being awake . . . forgetting and being asleep. My flesh wants to take plenty of naps. It wants to be babied. It wants to nod off. . . .

NO!

WAKE UP!

" . . . O sleeper, rise from the dead, and Christ will shine on you. Be very careful, then, how you live—not as unwise but as wise, making the most of every opportunity, because the days are evil" (Ephesians 5:14, 15).

Oh yes, I almost forgot. Two years ago our pipes froze, and in the ensuing repair and remodeling of the kitchen, eighteen old New England latches somehow got thrown out by mistake. So much for all my work and the sacrificial abandonment of my family. Maybe there's something about that I should wake up to.

Rake and stay awake.

Chapter Four
On My Own

. . . SO BLOW COLD WIND. TAKE these last dead leaves away, last vestiges of a former day. Let me know the barrenness; let me not cling to a few dried, shrunken memories, but let me find in the secret inner recesses the sap of faith—the strength and hope to live in the present. Let me find rugged life, surly life, deep-down-inside life where sap moves slow but sure, and hope holds steady to the promise of spring.

I've known your wind, O Spirit. I've heard that you blow wherever you please, that I cannot know where you come from or where you are going, though I hear your sound. I've always pictured you blowing through my leafy branches so all could see how I flicker in the sunlight. I never expected your wind would also carry this cold that now strips me bare, leaving me alone and unattractive. Is this also from your hand, O Spirit?

Then blow. I will stretch out my arms and take it full force, holding on to the ground. I will turn to my roots and learn anew what it is that will nourish and strengthen me in this winter. I will not run to memories of leaves now fallen, nor wish for buds that cannot be. Though I know the day of buds will come, it is not here and it is not now, and I can only find real life in the here and now.

Contrary to its appearance, the tree is not dead, nor is it sleeping. It has only drawn inside what it once waved in the wind on the tips of its wide green leaves. It's the same life, but known and experienced in another way.

This is the reason why I came to New England—that a California Christian might have his faith tested by a New England winter. Spiritually, it is as if it's winter all the time here. In this culture, faith is typically held quietly inside, like the sap of a winter tree. Not only does that make it hard to spot, it's harder to tell the difference between a live tree and a dead one when all the leaves are gone.

When we first moved here, we attended church thirty minutes and four towns away, where I knew the pastor, originally from California. That made the transition more palatable, but it didn't form any lasting bond. We soon found out that thirty minutes and four towns away in New England is the same as two states away anywhere else.

A half-hour drive to church is nothing in California. I know of people who drive twice that far, three or more times a week to attend a good church. That's because in California, the church *is* the community. It takes the place of what people are not experiencing in their own neighborhoods.

Commuter churches do not work here. You attend church in your neighborhood. Church is a part of the community experience. You attend the P.T.A. meeting, the Yankee Homecoming festivities in the summer, the annual town meeting, church on Sundays, and if you're a real "townie," the bi-weekly town meeting in the firehouse. (We can always tell which week of the month we're in because the Olde Newbury fire engine is pulled out of the station house late afternoon on meeting day and parked along the village's Upper Green.) That's the way it is in New England. Church, like everything else, is an integral part of community life. So when we found we did not fit into that life thirty minutes and four towns away, we decided to try a local church.

Disaster. We went to one of the historical churches in town, one of the oldest church buildings in America, but it seemed that it had been a couple hundred years since there had been any sign of life in this church. This tree was not just winter-dead, it was dead-dead. The ancient tilting gravestones you walked through to get to the front door were the first clue. The minister was the second—mounting an elevated pulpit that suspended his head as if it were in a time capsule. His mind and thoughts were equally suspended; as was his hair, suspended in a crimp where he must have slept on it the night before and left it that way, like the same crimp left in his words where he slept on his sermon.

Barely more than a handful of adults and senior citizens dotted the pews. One of them gave us a look of disdain, because we'd had the nerve to bring small children into such a place! But the feeling that most exemplified this experience was the one I had when an ashen-faced elderly gentleman led us to our seat and closed us in the pew. Yes, closed us in; there were dividers down the middle of each pew and on the aisle was a gate that closed with a latch on the outside. When he fastened the gate shut, I felt that we were being buried alive in a coffin. We walked out with a shudder that morning, through the crooked gravestones sticking up haphazardly on the front lawn, feeling very far from California and anything green.

So this was what we'd come to? Where there's no apparent difference between dead trees and live trees in winter, and where seeds lie dormant in the frozen earth? This was not to be a season of flourishing fellowship; this was to be a season of rooting deeper, of holding on and finding what is real. This was to be a season of finding what is mine. Not the spinning seeds and pollen grains of other trees carried by fragrant summer winds, but the only life to be found in winter—my own. My life, my sap, my source, my roots.

Blow, Spirit . . . wind . . . blow. The autumn winds of a fading generation have blown me to this cold rocky shore, and I want to know what life is here. Can it be so cold as to snuff the fire out, so dark as to extinguish the flame?

> We cannot kindle when we will
> The fire which in the heart resides,
> The spirit bloweth and is still,
> In mystery our soul abides.[1]

What *was* I looking for when we came here? Did I expect churches like the ones we'd left? Someone else to help keep this fire of faith alive in me?

No, I remind myself, I came here to find me. Not something outside me, but something inside. To find my own faith. No one can impart belief to another: doctrines, yes; testimonies, yes; but not *belief*. That must be a personal possession.

I know people who were raised with a strong faith, and who have chosen to walk away from it. And I know others who have come to a belief after years of vehement antagonism to faith. Regardless of the theological position with which we align ourselves, the workings of the Spirit of God and the will of the individual remain largely a mystery to us.

Yes, a godly environment is a great asset if it exposes you to the truth about God, but it can also be a liability in terms of a real personal response to Him. It is possible to be defined by your environment without ever making a personal choice in regards to it. Our most valuable God-given possession is our ability to choose. It is what sets us apart from the angels and the animals and enables us to have a real, honest-to-goodness, give-and-take relationship with God.

The fact that I have spent all my early years in the center of everything Christian doesn't mean that any right choices about God I may have made were obvious or any easier to make because of my environment. In retrospect, I am seeing that in some ways they were more difficult—easier

---

[1]Oswald Chambers, *My Utmost For His Highest*.

to confess, perhaps, but harder to confirm in their integrity.

A life lived in conformity to accepted beliefs always makes it debatable whether a choice has ever really been made in regard to those beliefs. The ugly duckling may have had to go through a great deal of soul searching and ridicule before he discovered he was a swan, but I doubt any of his nest-mates ever took the time to stare into the water and make any similar conclusions in regard to their duckiness.

Here in New England, I've come to realize that I have been staring at everyone else's Christian face for so long, I am no longer sure if it is my face or another's I wear. I grew up being taught that anything that had to do with *self* was wrong. It's still hard to say *mine*. It was hard for me to write those words: *my* life, *my* sap, *my* source, *my* roots. I still cringe every time I read it. I learned to look upon any form of the possessive as being suspect—until I came to wonder whose faith I had, mine or someone else's. Only then did I realize the question was too important to ignore.

Twelve years ago my wife and I walked out of our house in California to find that the nine year-old son of one of our best friends had graced the dirty window of our car with an important message about himself that he felt the world should know. With his finger he had boldly scrawled these three words: RODD IS GREAT.

Now Marti, whose pagan background is always clashing with my Christian one, immediately thought this was a great thing and I agreed—for a moment. But second thoughts and taped messages in my psyche soon crept in with their familiar warnings and accusations and bounced around in my brain. *This kid is going to have to be taken down before he ever discovers what spiritual greatness is. This really isn't good. He never learned the Sunday School song about putting yourself last.*

And around these thoughts, and looming even larger, were my feelings on the matter, which only now I begin to understand. I was actually mad at him, but not for writing on my car. I was mad with envy. I wanted to smash this little kid, or at least his ego. I might have owned the car, but this kid owned an ego. How come he got to have one and I didn't? Had I ever written JOHN IS GREAT on anything? Could I have? Why was this nine year old more proud of himself than I could ever remember being? Why did I want to take it away from him?

What is it about the Christian experience that negates ordinary human feelings and makes Christians appear to be so—what is it? Other-worldly at best; wimpy at worst. What is it that takes even ownership of our own faith away? Sometimes I wonder if, as a Christian, I've had all my parts connected up properly. In my case, I have learned to focus so much on what is *wrong* with me that I am often unable to see anything *right*. I feel like all the normal wires that connect will, mind, emotions and glands have all been pulled out of the switchboard for fear of one faulty connection.

Why is it that I am coming to a new conclusion?—that God would prefer to deal with one person, alive and fully connected up, than to have a thousand "surrendered" souls with their plugs pulled, rolling over and playing dead? Maybe this was what Martin Luther meant when he encouraged people to sin boldly if they were going to sin at all. At least that is better than an insipid weakness that masks as some kind of holy helplessness. God prefers a "hot" or a "cold" person to one who is "lukewarm"; and Paul desires a living sacrifice as opposed to a dead one.

Perhaps it was this that I envied in the nine-year-old son of a friend—a natural connection with his inner being that hadn't been tampered with by a predisposed Christianity. Surely there is a definite sacrifice involved in following Christ, a giving up of one's self. But don't you first have to possess a *self* in order to surrender it? It was that first possession that my particular brand of Christianity never allowed me to have. I'm sure I *had* a self—I just never got to enjoy it, to acknowledge it, to operate from it, to own myself or give myself away. And most certainly, not to display it publicly, on anyone's car window.

The conclusion is so obvious I missed it for years. If I was never allowed to possess my self, to be filled up with self, to be like a nine-year-old kid who thought he was God's answer to the world, then I never had anything real to give. I heard every Christian expectation; I obeyed them as best I could, but without being connected up inside like a normal person, I lived much of my spirituality in the abstract. I sinned in the abstract, I was forgiven in the abstract, I took on spiritual qualities in the abstract. I was a fundamental, Bible-believing, dedicated *abstract*.

I used to think that in order to show you were alive in Christ, you had to be green, all the time. The maple tree outside my window would not have had a place in my Christianity; Christians were evergreens. But the only way Christians can stay forever green is for Christianity to be artificial—to hide our human emotions, wants, or ambitions behind an artificial greenery of scripture quotes and Praise-the-Lords. And in doing so we become like artificial Christmas trees that stay green in the attic ready to spread their plastic-wound wiry branches the next time you bring them out. They may be green, but they are not alive. Artificial Christmas trees do what they are supposed to do, even bend to the desired shape, but they are not connected to anything real.

What is real is sometimes bony and bare, and scratches up against windows and walls. What is real is scrawled on dirty car windows by nine-year-olds. A real relationship with God is a give-and-take relationship between a man or a woman and the one who made and conceived them in His mind.

What's real is me on the wrestling mat with God, and God on the mat with me—facing each other alone.

Chapter Five
"I Will Not Let You Go. . . ."

IT SNOWED THIS MORNING, first snow this year. I had driving duty today, so I made the rounds on slushy roads amidst somewhat careless drivers reluctant to regain their snow-sense this early in November. Four houses and six kids later, we drove into the elementary school turnaround, with Alvin and the Chipmunks blaring their own kinetic brand of music on the car stereo. The kids were all slightly embarrassed, but I could tell they loved it.

"Okay everybody," I announced as I pulled up in front of the double doors. "We provided the snow and the Chipmunks music for this morning, the rest is up to you. Have a great day!" And as I watched them pile out of three doors and a hatchback, I wondered, *Is what happens today up to them? Is it up to me? How much of it?*

I wonder if God ever drives us up to the double doors of the rest of our lives and says, "Okay, I provided the cross, the resurrection, the Holy Spirit and the power—the rest is up to you. Have a great day!" And stepping out of the car, we approach those doors with all the apprehensions of a child. Would this mean He was abandoning me? No, probably no more than I abandoned my kids this morning by dropping them off at school. He would just be kicking me out of the house. Time to grow up.

But what's up to God and what's up to me? The pastor must wonder about this as he steps up to the pulpit, opens his Bible, and arranges his notes neatly in front of him. In the split-second between the time he opens his mouth and the words come out, does he wonder whose words they will be? The singer of spiritual songs must wonder about this as she finishes the song and sits down to the applause still ringing in her ears; were they touched by God or by her? I wonder about this as my kids struggle with the heavy double doors, getting all tangled up in backpacks, mittened-thumbs, and each other. *What's up to God, what's up to them? And as their father, what's up to me?*

I wonder about this as I drive back home on slippery roads still questioning whether this move to New England was the right thing. *Was it me or God that moved me here?*

Jacob wanted to know the answer to this same question when he discovered—after sweating, spitting blood and smarting from a hip dislocation—that lo and behold he had been rolling in the dirt all night with God. He hung in there because he wanted to know what was his own. He wanted to know if he had the blessing. He wanted to know if God was with him.

Ever since I first heard this story as a child, I've wondered why Jacob wrestled with God. It didn't seem right that a man should take on God in a wrestling match. Nor did it seem necessary, being that Jacob already possessed the very blessing over which he was fighting. Now it's finally clear to me what went on between Jacob and God that night. It's really no different than what I'm going through right now, trying to wrestle out, in my Christian experience, what is real and what is not—what is mine and what is God's.

This Jacob-heel-grabber, the one who had ahold of his brother's foot at birth and wouldn't let go until he got Esau to pawn off his birthright for a measly bowl of Campbell's— this same Jacob, when as a man he found out he had ahold of the foot of God, grabbed even harder, with all that he was in that moment, and cried, "I will not let you go unless you bless me!" This has special meaning, considering he already *had* the blessing. He had aced his brother out of that too, by tricking Isaac into thinking that he, Jacob, was really Esau, the firstborn, the hairy hunter, the one Isaac was intending to bless. You could say that Jacob, when he finally landed in the ring with God, was simply demanding from God what was already his, but had been ill-gotten.

This part I understand. I know what it's like to possess a blessing and wonder if it is really mine. (Was this pre-arranged? Did my mother have anything to do with this? Was I myself when I got it, or was I trying to be someone else?) Is this blessing *mine*—would I wrestle anyone for it—or did it fall into my lap with my name on it?

I know what it's like to be a Christian and not to be sure how you got it. I know what it's like to envy hairy guys, like Esau, who go out and hunt and grunt and get what they get. I know what it's like to have aced them out of the blessing and then stand around them with smooth skin, feeling a bit dishonest and slightly in danger.

For that reason I understand why, when Jacob realized he had God on the mat, he held on for dear life. It was *his* life. This was his chance to make sure about this blessing thing—not the blessing he and his mother manipulated, the one he tricked his father out of. *This is me, Jacob, the smooth guy, wearing my own clothes, and I want the real blessing.*

Is this okay? Can someone meet God like this? Will God go to the mat with a person? Has He given us that much personal integrity?

Up until recently, if I had found myself in a situation similar to Jacob's, I would have behaved in an entirely different manner. I wouldn't have wrestled with the man in the first place. I've never been in a physical fight in my life. I'm a smooth man; fights are for hairy guys. Something must have happened during Jacob's twenty years in Paddan Aram that put some hair on his chest. I would have asked the man what he wanted from me and tried to avoid a fight.

Secondly, had I somehow gotten the nerve to wrestle the man, I would have had a completely different reaction upon finding it was *God* I'd had ahold of all night. I would have released my grip, jumped back and cried, "Ooops! I didn't know it was You! Oh my goodness, have I done something wrong? Why didn't you tell me?"

I, too, want my own blessing—my own handle on a relationship with God. But my understanding is cluttered with so many slogans and formulas. . . . Do you tithe for this blessing? Do you claim it after naming it? Do you get it when you give up? Do you let go and let God, or do you let God let go? So many seminars, so many sermons, so many slogans piled up one on top of another in my brain . . . like so many autumn leaves piled up in November.

Except that now, for the first time, if God turned up one night in this cold barren place, I think I'd grab Him and hold on just like Jacob. Yes, I think I would grab on. . . .

It's taken me a long time to get smart enough to do this—what should have been a normal human response. And I, like Jacob, had to leave my hometown and go out to another land, where blessings don't come through gerrymandering in your father's tent, but through the hard work of your own hands. Jacob had to fall in love with Rachel and work seven years in order to earn the first thing in the world he really wanted—the right to make her his wife. Then on Jacob's wedding night, his father-in-law gave him a piece of his own crafty medicine and slipped Rachel's sister, Leah, into his bed instead. But Jacob turned right around, went back into the fields, and worked for seven more years. So by the time he had his bout with God, Jacob was the proud owner of two wives, eleven sons, many servants and much cattle and livestock, all of which he rightfully earned from Laban.

Like Jacob, I grew up where life was already arranged in the shape of a blessing. I came close to disdaining my faith because of this. Like Jacob, I have had to leave in order to possess the blessing. And like Jacob, the love of a beautiful woman has had something to do with this spiritual struggle.

When I met Marti in 1974, she was in charge of the Fellowship of Christian Airline Personnel (FCAP) in Los Angeles. She had been responsible for forming the L.A. chapter of this organization and building it to a membership of over 500. She had been a Christian for only one year.

On the night I met her, she told me how she had organized evangelistic banquets, brought in speakers and singers such as Hal Lindsay, Lane Adams, and Barry McGuire, and watched hundreds of airline people come to Christ and join FCAP. Then she told me how she began teaching a Bible study for 90 flight attendants and prepared for it by listening to a radio preacher every week. How she and another Christian flight attendant would bid for trips together, and then pray for at least one non-Christian to tell about Christ and one Christian to encourage on each flight, and how God had answered every one of those many prayers. How she would speak in churches sashaying irreverently to the pulpit, brandishing a mink stole, a cocktail glass, and a cigarette holder saying, "I suppose you thought this was what a stewardess was like" (this was when they were still called "stewardesses," not "flight attendants"), and then proceed to give her testimony. How after all this, she was getting a little burned-out and simply wished for one standing ovation. So right there, in a quaint little restaurant nestled in the hills above Santa Cruz, I had granted her wish, sending her under the table immediately.

It was humorous then, but I realize now that lonely handclap was all the recognition I ever gave her for all that she had done and all that God had done in and through her. She hadn't been around Christians long enough to get messed up about what was hers, and what was God's. She just went to work with everything she had.

I was joking when I clapped. I was making a mockery of human activity that, in my superior spiritual knowledge, was suspect. This was because back then, I was smart: I knew a lot more than I know now about what's up to me and what's up to God. This was back when the tree had lots of green leaves on its branches. Upon hearing Marti's story, I had concluded that she hadn't been a Christian long enough to know how to do all this stuff "in the Spirit," so this activity had all been Marti acting "in the flesh"—and it was nice and God would probably figure out some way to use it. But for now, she had better get out of the ministry business. That was *my* department. So after we got married and she asked me in essence, "What now with my life?" I told her she needed to put herself on the shelf for a while. She needed to "die" before God could create anything good in her.

It's not that Marti hadn't been a Christian long enough; it's that I had been an abstract Christian too long without doing much more than think about it. I used to think Jacob was audacious in wrestling with God. Yet here I was having the audacity to play God in my wife's life, telling her when to die and when to live as if I were the bearer of death and life.

Which is worse—wrestling with God, or playing God?

Unlike Jacob and Rachel, I didn't have to work to get Marti, I've had to work to *keep* her—or, I should say, to *keep up* with her. Marti hasn't had a prearranged, blessing-shaped world to grow up in. She has always met life head on, as it comes to her. She doesn't get stuck wondering what's up to her and what's up to God. No one got ahold of her head and tampered with her spiritual plugs—though I tried at first, she wouldn't have it. (She will wrestle with me, too.)

Marti works out from her real self and like Rodd and Jacob, is probably wrestling with God in some form on a regular basis. In the midst of this, she is dealing with a real Holy Spirit and obeying Him, when she's sure it's Him. To my wonder and chagrin, God continues to meet her at this level.

This, to me, is the most overwhelming thing about the one who becomes a Jacob and chooses to wrestle with God—not that we would have the nerve to do such a thing, but that God would have the grace to meet us on our level, and wrestle with us.

I wonder now: Does He love *me* that much? I will not let Him go this time, until I know.

Chapter Six
Destiny Calls

ACROSS THE SNOW-DUSTED YARD, beyond my maple tree, is a long driveway to our neighbors' house. This time of year, when the trees and bushes are bare, I can see their side porch, where we sit and visit on summer evenings. I can also see the poles they drove into the ground along the driveway before the earth froze up, to mark its edges for plowing when the snow falls heavily. Since we've been here, we haven't had a major storm, such as the northeast is capable of producing, but everyone still talks of the Blizzard of '78 that dropped three feet of snow in a day, stranding people in their homes and commuters in their offices in Boston for a whole weekend.

The family that lives in the house next door is an extended one: Malcolm and Alcena, the grandparents, live downstairs; their daughter Debbie lives upstairs with her husband and two children. It's primarily a matriarchal setup. Malcolm is retired and in ill-health; Chuck, the son-in-law, works hard and when he's not working, he plays hard on various sports teams, depending on the season, so that he is largely absent from the household. Chuck and Esau have a lot in common—both of them "hairy" men, frequently off hunting in their own ways. Mother and daughter hold down the fort.

A major duty in holding down that fort includes a nursery school that Debbie and Alcena operate together out of the front corner room of the house. A number of people my age, who grew up in Newbury, remember going there almost forty years ago. Every morning at nine and every afternoon at four, car wheels crackle up and down the gravel drive and mother and daughter chat with the parents in voices that skip brightly through the trees.

"Hi, how was your weekend?" or "Can you believe this weather?" are the kind of things I can hear on a typical morning, except the word is "weath-ah," because in Massachusetts that's the way it should sound. So my son, "Christoph-ah," had his first schooling experience next door at Alcena's nursery school.

My first few weeks in New England found me often at their house, borrowing tools, asking directions, and inquiring about water hook-ups, leach fields, power outages, storm windows, coming snowstorms. I knew nothing about such things, but now they were my immediate concern as a New England homeowner. They were thoroughly kind and patient with me, doing away with the myth of Yankee "coldness" that I'd expected from both hearsay and some previous experience.

Malcolm was especially helpful in this regard, being a retired contractor with first-hand experience with many of the houses in the area. He was also a personal history book of the neighborhood, and my afternoon breaks were filled with colorful stories about old roads, out-dated property lines and lives now only living in his memory.

It was Malcolm who first told me about the Frosts, the original builders and owners of 24 Green Street, a childless couple who lived here for forty years. They passed away five years before we arrived. Malcolm and his contemporaries still refer to our house as "the Frost home." It was Malcolm who told me how Mrs. Frost used to teach piano lessons in the front room and was always excusing herself to the bathroom for a nip from her private flask. It was Malcolm who told me how Mrs. Frost was a perfectionistic housekeeper who had the wood floors waxed every week, and when she and Mr. Frost had lobster, almost every Saturday night, they would eat it standing over the kitchen sink so as not to make a mess on the kitchen table. It was Malcolm who told me that the small rise in our backyard used to be a road that brought the milkman up to their property, and the ball diamond on the Green used to be a communal cow pasture.

Malcolm seemed to love to have someone interested in all this, as if it took someone from the outside to come in and appreciate it. He talked as if he were telling me things he felt no one else wanted to know, and he was probably right. Even in New England, appreciation for the past is giving way to the encroaching boundaries of "yuppiedom." There certainly have been no other people I know of interested in listening to an old man emphysemically wheeze his way through a history of his changing neighborhood. These little chats were very important to him.

They were important to me, too. We came here to New England to be involved in a community, and we have been received by this family with great sincerity. It's true there is a definite aloofness on the surface with many New Englanders. But the minute they realize you genuinely want to commit yourself to a relationship, I've found New Englanders respond with great loyalty.

Not to mention the fact that in Malcolm's cellar is every tool I could ever want, need, or imagine. Malcolm must chuckle often behind my back as I walk off with a crowbar or a sledgehammer and cement chisel with which to tear out the tiles in my bathroom or to pound a hole in the concrete cellar wall so I can pump out the water that floods in. He must wonder what brought this greenhorn Californian out here to such an old land, among such hearty stock. He must wonder, at times, if we will make it, and for how long.

His son-in-law, Chuck, is a sports enthusiast, as I've

said, and a big physical man who doesn't talk much. This time of year the sport is hockey, and the local rink is in such demand that he can often be heard heading out at eleven or twelve o'clock at night for the only available ice time. Later on in winter it will be basketball. Then, when first buds form and the small lake from the spring thaw finally dries up in the center of the softball diamond at the lower end of the Green, across from our house, it will be the punch of ball-in-glove and loud cries from the players every Tuesday and Thursday night all summer long.

None of Chuck's lifestyle do I envy—except for the softball. Often, I've been working in the front yard trying unsuccessfully to ignore the yells from the field and the *thwack* of the bat. I love playing ball! I love to watch baseball, to follow a team through the season from spring training to the dregs of October; I'm a frustrated sportswriter at heart. But most of all I love to play baseball on an organized team. Actually "love" is inadequate to express how I feel about this. In classic Greek terms, *eros* is more appropriate. My most recurring nightmare is a dream where I am trying to get to a game to play shortstop and I forget my glove, have to return home for it, and never make it to the game. I hate that dream!

The team Chuck plays on is the Olde Newbury Clammers, made up of neighborhood players. It is run by a couple guys who operate the Citgo station across the street from the Town Hall. The station acts as Gossip Central for the town of Newbury as well as being the headquarters of the Olde Newbury Clammers.

The year we moved into our house on Green Street in June, the current ball season was in full swing, so to speak. I was elated to discover an organized neighborhood team in existence right across the street. Surely this was God's provision for my every need! How could I *not* qualify? I knew I could play, and my house was right across the street from the ball diamond, for heaven's sake. Maybe now, I could finally be rid of that nasty nightmare.

It wasn't that easy.

I talked to Chuck about joining the team. Chuck shrugged and told me to go talk to Jimmy at the Citgo station. So I talked to Jimmy. Jimmy shrugged and told me they didn't really need any players, but if I wanted to show up I might be able to play if someone didn't happen to make it that night.

So I showed up. Twice. Everybody showed. Not only that, but I stood around feeling very smooth among a whole bunch of hairy guys. I tried a few more times that first year, and then gave it up.

Two years ago I almost got my chance for a debut. Marti had a writing assignment for her adult degree program to do a story on her neighborhood, so she chose to write an article about the Olde Newbury Clammers called, "Where the Boys Are," an appropriate title, I thought. Part of this project included some action pictures and coverage of a game. I decided to accompany her and, trying not to think much of it, I grabbed my glove on the way out. Just in case.

Once again, everybody showed. I did notice, however, that the shortstop was in knee-braces, his ability to run or move noticeably impaired. I kept a close eye on his activity while Marti snapped pictures. Halfway through the game the shortstop took a real shot, a line drive in the gut that dropped him right to his ailing knees. *Ha!*—I thought, reaching for my glove—*destiny calls!*

The whole team gathered around him for four or five minutes. His wife went out to check on him. My heart picked up its beat and I thought of my dream. This was it—I had my glove, I didn't have to go back for it. I was about to show these guys I could play circles around them. I stood quietly under the trees in back of third base slamming a fist into my glove. Marti looked over at me, rolled her eyes, and snapped more pictures of the infield medical team.

A few minutes later they all dispersed, leaving our hero barely standing—*but still in the game!* The guy hobbled through the remainder of the evening. Two grounders went right by him at short, and when he hit, someone ran for

him. Through this entire ordeal, no one from the Olde
Newbury Clammers ever looked over at me. Not even once.

Now the summers go by with the *thwacks* and cheers of
so many Esaus reveling in their birthrights, while I work
on my lawn, polish the car—or the top of the barbecue, or
any other smooth surfaces I can find.

After six years my friends here are few. No one seems
to want me on their team. I never was able to develop any
kind of relationship with Chuck, his world is so far away
from mine. The one exception was when Alcena died, and
he came over to tell me in person and cried on my shoulder.

Thus the presence of real friends has been another part
of my life that this New England experience has stripped
away. My relationship with Malcolm hardly qualifies. Our
relationship has remained one of sharing the odd opposites
of our lives—like opposite ends of a generation, or a con-
tinent. We only meet because our extreme differences have
bent around and touched each other.

So I have drawn into myself and remained more alone
than I have been in other seasons of my life. This is partly
due to the lack of relationships that come from being heavily involved in a local church. Also to the fact that I have
not sought out relationships, at least not the kind I have
been used to—Christian relationships with Christian
friends for spiritual encouragement and the familiarity of
communication, background and mutually held beliefs.
No, I left that behind when I crossed the line somewhere
on I–80 midway through Nebraska. This, too, was an important leaving.

There are certain givens in a Christian relationship that
make for a comfortable environment for exchange. Christian relationships are generally non-threatening to me. Relationships with non-Christians, on the other hand, pose
a real challenge. I find myself digging around for a common
root, and failing to come up with one, where I'm used to
finding it—in a common system of beliefs—I am forced to
uncover new commonalities. Surprisingly, I have missed
the obvious commonalities in our basic humanity, because

I have been so spiritually minded. The good part of this loneliness is that it has forced me to relate with non-Christians, and in doing so I have discovered things about myself that I had not seen before.

Having always seen myself in an *us/them* relationship, I have tended to deal with non-Christians as being entirely unlike me. They were "them," we were "us," and the twain must never meet except in evangelistic settings. A non-Christian, to me, has been, for the most part, something akin to a martian.

I'm now seeing the negative effects of this "separation mentality" on me. For if they were unlike me, then I was unlike them, unable to find anything in our mutual human make-up worth sharing. The key word here is *worth*. If I reject the basic humanity of others, then there is something about my self I am missing. My refusal to relate to non-Christians may well signal an inability, or perhaps a reluctance to relate to myself and my own humanity in some way.

How often have I heard this kind of comment from other Christians: "I don't really enjoy being around non-Christians. There's really nothing to talk about. We have so little in common." *So little in common.* Really? You mean you've never fallen in love? Never yelled at a ball game? Never tried to go to the bathroom but couldn't because there were too many people in line? Never wished someone would just hold you? Never wanted to have sex? Never craved an ice cream cone on a hot day? Never wondered if you were the only one who didn't know what was going on?

This inability to relate is another one of those disconnected wires I've lived with all my Christian life. The wire that plugs us into our basic humanity is often tampered with, by both faulty theology and by our own reluctance to deal honestly with ourselves.

Building honest relationships—first with God and our *self*, then with others—is hard. It requires going deeper, stripping away old "spiritualized" resistances, getting to the heart level.

I know this will not be easy. Without my spiritual trappings, nobody seems to want me on their team. But I also know I must reach into the depths this time.

Chapter Seven
Into the Deep

ONE OF MY CALIFORNIA friends who over the years has resisted spiritual and emotional shallowness is Jack Joseph Puig, a brilliant recording engineer and producer who has worked on a number of my albums. He will not let me go, I say, until the roughness is gone from my music and the right qualities are there.

"Rip my heart out and throw it on the floor," says Jack sometimes as we play back a successful take in the studio. It's one of his favorite expressions, meaning that I've finally got the right combination of musical clarity and emotional honesty. Jack is a meticulous expert, continually on a crash course with his own kinetic energy, who knows you cannot engineer certain qualities into a song. The musician has to grope deep inside and tear them out from the depths.

As long as I've known Jack, most everything about him has been alive and kinetic. He has always worn his hair long in the back, falling over his shoulders. One of his dramatic gestures, when he's simultaneously "tired-but-wired" because of a long, late-night session in the studio, is to grab his long hair in the back and gently lift himself up off his seat, as if to physically drag himself into the fray.

"Wake up, Jack. Come on, Jack. Get going!" he shouts.

Sometimes I have to drag myself into consciousness, into battle with certain emotions that would keep me back from life—keep me small . . . disengaged. . . .

The clock radio woke me up this morning with James Taylor and Richard Souther singing "It Used To Be Her Town." The first four lines were perfect for me this morning. Something about being afraid of the knock on the door, being afraid to go out, being afraid to do anything where there might be even a shade of a doubt. She's locked herself in her little world.

That's me. A pushover to doubt and fear, I'm like the woman in the song: merely a shade of a doubt will stop me.

And unfortunately, I find that doubt and fear paralyze me over and over again. So it's not just a matter of being awakened by someone else—like when my three high school buddies first showed me an unhappy side of myself. *It is a matter of learning how to stay awake*—learning what it is inside me that wants to pull self-deception over me like a blanket and go back to sleep.

This is an urgent need—to stay awake—because I can fall asleep without even thinking: I come to an impasse— a task that has a fear attached to it, or a step I don't entirely know how to take—and I hesitate. And then I either grab my hair and pull myself through, or more often I pull back and find some handy way to distract myself. This is the danger zone for me, because when I pull back in one thing, I give in to the fear, and giving in to the fear is the same as feeding it. And the more I hold back, the more fear grows, until it fills up the whole area around me. Fear, for me, is one of the most common doorways out of the place of power with God.

Even as I write this, I can hear the voices crying in my

head, "John, you're forgetting about spiritual warfare. If fear is all around you, you'd better get down on your knees and pray against it. Didn't you read *This Present Darkness*?" I actually think that if I cried out to God to deliver me from *this* fear, He might respond with something like, "Hey, don't whine to me about this. You walked into this fear yourself. You'll have to walk out. I'm over here waiting for you on the other side of it."

Praying and asking God to remove fear that is the result of my refusal to step out in faith seems a little like building my house on sand and then asking God to protect me from the storm. He's already told me how to get rid of fear: step into love, because perfect love casts out all fear. Sitting here choking on my own fear—backing away from the challenge, finding some old New England latches to restore in the meantime—is *not* loving God, myself or my wife and family. It is loving my own brown-brittle self with all its green chlorophyll drained. It is loving the fact that I don't have to do anything but sit here and be afraid. I must like this place or I wouldn't spend so much time here; it provides me with an excuse for doing nothing but justifying my paralysis.

How many times does this happen to me?

I ended the day yesterday pulling wallpaper off the walls of my daughter's room. Not that there was anything wrong with that; it was part of my original plan for the evening. It's just that—it's about the *only* part of my plan yesterday that I put into action. And—Wow! *You can imagine how much courage that took!* When my wife returned from her day, I might as well have been wrapped up in old sticky wallpaper in a fetal position, sucking my thumb. She needed me, but I was not good to her in terms of the plans, and decisions, and directions required—the many things that would have been the rewards of my day, had I spent it more wisely. It was me, lost once again in the kitchen cupboard latches, afraid to face real, hard decisions. When the green stuff drains out, the leaf will show its true colors . . . always . . . count on it.

My wife sees me on stage and marvels at the power and the confidence—and yet she wonders why that power doesn't always accompany her home. It's because I can get the truth, and say it, but I may or may not believe it for myself. May not believe enough, that is, to act on it.

Yes, God does hear me, even when I pray in fear. He does speak—not to the fear, but to me. I believe He's telling me how silly it is to ask Him to rescue me this time. Usually my prayer is "Either fix things, God, or take me away from here." If I had one shred of the real sense of the fear of God, I would be zapped on the spot. "Fix it . . . or take me away. . . ." *Neither option asks anything of me.*

When I read, in Acts, about Paul's conversion, I envy that he got a direct vision, a heavenly voice and a visit from a total stranger to authenticate his experience. I envy the miracle. What I sometimes forget to note is that he was stricken blind. And when the word of God came to him later through Ananias it went like this: "This man Paul is my chosen instrument, to carry my name before Gentiles and their kings and before the people of Israel. I will show him how much he must suffer for my name."

Suffer? Wait a minute, what happened to the miracle? Who said anything about suffering? What happened to my rescue?

Is God interested in rescuing the flesh? Is He going to perform a miracle of resurrection on a few dead leaves? Why am I looking for short cuts around the process of dying to these old habits and manipulations? I am wishing to be robed so soon in the blooming garb of spring without going through the winter that must come in between. But there must first come the vulnerability of being stripped bare, of waiting, of knowing that only He can produce life out of this death, of hoping in a life I know is in me by faith, though it does not now appear on my branches.

And what do I do in the meantime? Do I hibernate through the winter and wait for the huge movements of the earth to put the sun in a better place for me? It's winter for me, but life still goes on for everyone around me. My wife needs me. My children need me. The audiences I stand before need me. They need me to walk through and out of this flesh that keeps me trapped in my fear—trapped in my self.

God, I believe, needs me too. He will not deliver me from a fear behind which I choose to cower.

"Wake up, John. Come on . . . get going!"

This is what I've come to see: John Fischer long ago got used to falling asleep at the spiritual wheel; he got used to cruising along on other people's energy; he got used to . . .

"Wake up, John!"

Okay, I hear you. Like Jack, I'm grabbing the hair on the back of my neck, gently lifting myself off my seat.

> I have crossed the chasms of my casual crimes
> I have passed the sign at least a thousand times
> Waiting for a hand to rescue me
> While at any time I could have walked out free
> My ship is in, my debt is due
> The time is now: time for you.

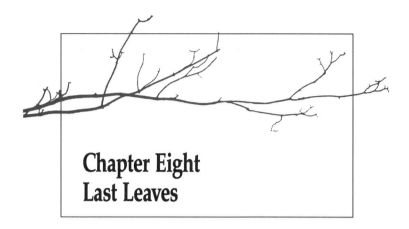

Chapter Eight
Last Leaves

IT FINALLY HAPPENED. A HUNGRY northeast wind (they call them "nor'easters") blew on by here and picked clean the carcass of a tree. The last two leaves must have let go somewhere in the night; nothing but dark, wet, twisted branches left.

What did these last leaves represent? I think of them as remnants of a seasonless Christianity. Last notions of a false religion. Stubborn hangers-on. In many ways they are spiritual myths and to follow them—to be governed in my thinking and feelings by dead, shriveled-up beliefs—is to find myself more superstitious than spiritual. I believe I would be astonished to find how much superstition there is in many of the so-called spiritual ideas that float around in my brain.

Here's one: "Do the right thing and all will go well." This is a dangerous myth that can trap on either side of its equation. If things are going well, then I can assume I'm doing it right and there is no need to be alert to God or to my responsibilities. If things are going poorly, then I must constantly rake through the surface of my intents and actions, looking for the cause of my unfortunate circumstances.

I have believed, with all my heart, that the move east was "the right thing," but all has not gone well. My life in New England hasn't turned out to be at all what I hoped.

I came, in part, to uncover "a whole new audience for my music," one which no one could ever find unless they lived here. The musical directions I took as a result of being here—though they've been extremely fulfilling to me personally—never have translated into concerts and album sales.

I also knew it was "the right thing" to reach back musically to some real rock-'n-roll roots, and to form a small band to help me play this new/old music. Few will ever know of the concerts like the one we played in Athol, Massachusetts, where a young Christian couple sold a field to finance a Christian festival for their community. No more than seventy-five people were there—but all seventy-five of them were dancing in the rain for the last five songs. At the end, the sponsor counted out $1500 in cash and told me, his face still wet from the rain, that the experience was worth every penny.

Did I do the right thing? Was there measurable success? Not by the standards of the Christian music "industry." Not by west coast standards. For a while, we couldn't pay our bills and, at one point, we almost lost our house. If I were living by this maxim, "Do the right thing, and all will go well," I would be constantly tormented with self-doubt and condemnation. Things have not gone well for a long time.

And that is not to take anything away from doing the right thing. A righteous heart—a heart that's been set free by Jesus Christ—always wants to do what's right. But there's no guarantee concerning what will come after. Do the right thing and you may lose a job, a friend, or a contract. There were a number of saints in church history who did the right thing and lost their heads. Jesus did the right thing and got crucified.

Sometimes I've forgotten to stay awake, and wound up looking at someone else's success as a sign that they're doing it right and I'm not, or at least doing it more correctly than I, since I am less successful. This is the kind of thinking that weakens my own sense of grace and calling and causes me to be intimidated by others. Why is it that I immediately assume that a Christian businessman who has more money than I do and seems to have everything under control in his life is necessarily more spiritual than I, and that I should place myself and my own insight from God in a lesser light? Because, according to the myth, if I was doing the right thing, all would go better for me, too.

This myth—this dead leaf—creates spiritual competition between individuals and ruins the possibility of true relationships. I recently spoke at length with Larry Norman while we were attending a Christian music festival in Europe. Even though Larry and I both helped to innovate contemporary Christian music at the same time with much the same vision, we've never gotten very close over these years. Only casual encounters. One reason, I now know, is that I've always been afraid of Larry—intimidated by his unabashed prophetic voice and his wacky John-the-Baptist ability to stay a real "Jesus freak" over all these years. I've always assumed this was because he was closer to God than I was, and closer to what he should be doing. He was certainly more successful than I: He had his own record company—that should say a lot right there. Then I would hear rumors about a personal problem, or an unsuccessful business dealing and say to myself, *See, he's really not any closer to God than I am.*

Imagine my surprise when he told me during a concert producer's barbecue in a backyard in Norway that he had always been intimidated by me—that he envied my ability to fill a page in *Contemporary Christian Music* magazine every month with something that sounded like it was right from God. He always thought that I walked around with a direct link to the Throne—that at anytime I wanted I could beam up and—"*Zap*"—truth would come to me. There we were, each punishing ourselves for the other's blessing.

As we talked, we discovered that each of our lives was filled with plenty of mistakes—and yet an abundance of the grace of God, too.

"Do the right thing, and all will go well." This is a hard leaf to let go. It offers so many great excuses for inactivity. If things are going well, I am excused from checking my actions, since I must be doing the right things already. And if things are going poorly, I can render myself inactive in other ways. For one thing, I can blame God for not showing me what I'm doing wrong, and excuse myself in the meantime from doing anything until He does. This thinking becomes even more twisted when applied to someone else. In my childhood home as I was growing up, we used to think that if someone was better-off than us, there had to be something secretly wrong with them. God couldn't possibly be blessing them more than He was blessing us. There was undoubtedly something wrong with their riches and, besides, we were sacrificing for the ministry and God had a special place in His heart for us.

Some people are powerful enough to manipulate circumstances so that they can hold on to this dead leaf a long time—constantly telling themselves they must be doing it right because things are going well. Perhaps they can engineer a promotion or buy their way into a good school. Or for those who do not possess the means to manipulate reality, fantasy is attractive. As long as the mere image of success can be maintained, then I can delude myself and others into believing I must be doing the right thing.

I'm certain this kind of delusion was prevalent in the personal justification of the well-publicized sins of TV evangelists. How could these people continue to live with greater and greater moral failure, while continuing with their ministries? What rationalizations would allow this contradiction to exist in their minds? It seems that, as long as the money kept coming in, they were "successful." And as long as they were successful in this material way, they took it as a sign of God's blessing. So they must be doing the right thing. If God continued to bless them in spite of their sin, He must have found a way to allow their sin, look the other way, or cater to their weakness since they were so indispensable in His kingdom.

In short, it seems to have come down to the false belief that the blood of Jesus *covers up* sin—rather than the truth, which is that His blood makes it possible for us to come before God and freely admit we need new life within in order to overcome our old dead sins. . . .

Recently, I was meditating on the baptism of Jesus, and specifically on this scripture: "As Jesus was coming up out of the water, he saw heaven being torn open and the Spirit descending on him like a dove. And a voice came from heaven: 'You are my Son, whom I love; with you I am well pleased' " (Mark 1:10, 11).

The Son of God wades slowly out into the Jordan River, placing himself in the hands of a rough wilderness preacher. Crossing His hands over His chest, He becomes vulnerable in the arms of John. He falls back into the water, being held down for a catch of a breath, and then breaks the surface of the Jordan, His head cradled in the Baptist's arms with water raining off His face, hair and beard. His eyes turn upward, water still dropping from his lashes. A dove circles in the air. And out of the sky comes a voice— a proclamation of acceptance and love—"My Son, whom I love, with you I am well pleased."

This is the beginning of Jesus' earthly ministry, though He has yet to do any *work* of ministry. No one has been healed, no one raised from the dead, no sermons, no multitudes fed. Yet here is a proclamation from heaven—a decree from the throne of God while His Son stands dripping wet in the arms of John. It is not the result of any activity of Jesus; it is the relationship out of which that activity will spring. It is the announcement of Jesus' right-standing with the Father. It was Jesus' beginning and I believe it's where we begin, as well.

Everything begins here. Imagine what we would be like if our earthly fathers had started us out like this: "My son/ daughter, whom I love—with you I am well pleased." Most of us, instead, are traveling through acres of pain trying to perform the right way and earn an acceptance that never comes. For some, it is almost impossible to conceive of this—an acceptance that has nothing to do with what we do or don't do.

Yet with God, our heavenly Father, all things are possible, and this is exactly the impossible truth we must begin to believe for ourselves: that we too receive this proclamation of acceptance when our new life in Jesus begins. This is what the birth, baptism, life, death and resurrection of Jesus Christ has made possible for all of us. You and I are well-pleasing to God. Our acceptance is not based upon our performance, but upon what Christ has already accomplished for us.

God's forgiveness is a free-flowing fountain spilling out from the cross. His acceptance of me is a given. It was spoken over me when He put away sin forever through the death of His own Son. His acceptance of me is not something I can create or destroy by my actions or lack of them; it is a fountain into which I plunge or I do not.

> There is a fountain filled with blood
> Drawn from Immanuel's veins,
> And sinners plunged beneath that flood
> Lose all their guilty stains.[3]

Either I wake up in the morning and look at the mirror and see in my unshaven face God's son whom He loves, with whom He is well pleased, or I forget what it is that I see in that mirror, or I don't see anything at all. Believe it or don't believe it, those are our only options. Doing the right thing so God will accept me is an oxymoron—it doesn't make sense to the truth. What makes sense to the truth is: God has already accepted me, so I can do the right thing.

Something so wonderful should be easy to accept, and yet receiving something for nothing goes against every fi-

---

[3]William Cowper, "There Is a Fountain."

ber of human flesh. We want to believe God has given us a gift, and yet we don't. We hang on to our shriveled up, dead self-righteousness and self-justification because it's all we have ever known. We have existed on a *performance basis* from the cradle. We're not about to let go of it without a fight—without a long night's wrestling match on a stream-bank in a private wilderness. The stubborn human will is both my friend and my foe: When I'm holding on to God, it is my friend; when I am holding on to anything else, it is my enemy.

"I am acceptable to God." *Think of it*. This is the beginning, out of which good works can flow from my life. I am not trying to prove anything; I am walking in what has already been proven. God has proven His pleasure in me by dying for me and removing the barrier to His acceptance, which was my sin.

> My sin—O the bliss of this glorious thought—
> My sin, not in part, but the whole,
> Is nailed to the cross, and I bear it no more:
> Praise the Lord, praise the Lord, O my soul![4]

Tape it on your mirror—paste it on the ceiling over your bed so it's the first thing you see in the morning: "I am acceptable to God." As I sit here right now, all my branches feeling barren—I am acceptable to God. It's not because of what I'm doing, not because I'm in the flow or in the know—definitely not because my branches are full and green. It's because of what Christ has done for me and what I know deep down in my roots: I am acceptable to God.

Odd, that a leafless tree could find itself so appealing.

I look at this bare tree out my window and suddenly it's not as bad as it seems. The hundreds of thousands of leaves that in June formed the huge, glorious bulk of its shape will turn into nothing more than 20 full plastic bags come March, when the snow melts and I finally finish raking them all up. And in spite of this present barrenness

---

[4]Horatio G. Spafford, "It Is Well With My Soul."

they will be back, and even their leaving is always a blaze of fiery color worthy of celebration. The leaves, like seasons and circumstances, come and go, but the strength of the tree remains in its branches, its trunk, and its roots. This tree, however barren it may appear now, is an integral part of all things strong and growing.

> So I stand here still believing
> Wanting not for buds of spring,
> Nor waving in the winds of memory
> Corpses that no longer sing;
> But letting go of false delusions,
> Stripped of all that had to die,
> Throwing bare arms up to heaven,
> I hug the earth and breathe the sky.

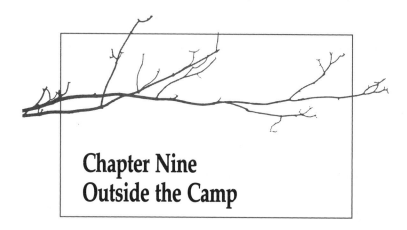

Chapter Nine
Outside the Camp

IN THE DEAD OF WINTER, I returned from a weekend trip to find that Marti had signed me up for a rather bizarre proposition. This, in itself, was nothing new. I get volunteered for all kinds of interesting activities this way.

At a neighborhood party she attended alone in my absence, a discussion arose with two male friends in our community about the distance most men in our society keep between themselves. Most men hide behind what they do, and rarely have a relationship purely for the companionship. One of these men was daring enough to admit this deficiency to my wife.

Now you have to understand that Marti is a *put-it-together* kind of person. You don't discuss "possibilities" with Marti. It is simply not in her character to window-shop. Marti gets things done; and if you make the mistake of dropping a casual idea in her vicinity, she will turn it into an event before you have time to turn around. Or, as in this case, if you even mention a need, she will come up with both the idea *and* the event.

Marti suggested that these two men and I should spend not a lunch, not an evening, but a whole weekend together, with no agenda except to get to know each other and to become friends. By the time I returned home and heard about this encounter, I already had an assignment to set this thing up.

I probably should mention, at this point, that neither of these men are born-again Christians. This may not seem like a big deal to many people, but to me it was monumental. To spend a whole weekend with *two* of them, would be . . . well . . . what would we have in common?

I bravely decided that this is New England, where much of my former life has been stripped away. Then I was ready for the encounter—yes, even excited about it. And frightened: behold, yet another real line to cross.

Before calling these guys, though, I had some wrestling to do. Wasn't it true that Christians are not supposed to have friendships with non-Christians? "What fellowship hath light with darkness?" and "Don't you know that friendship with the world is enmity with God" and "Love not the world, neither the things that are in the world. . . ."

The most direct reference I know of that contradicts this *keep-away-to-keep-pure* form of thinking is in 1 Corinthians 5:9–12. "I have written you in my letter not to associate with sexually immoral people—not at all meaning the people of this world who are immoral, or the greedy and swindlers, or idolaters. *In that case you would have to leave this world* [italics mine]. But now I am writing you that you must not associate with anyone who calls himself a brother but is sexually immoral or greedy, an idolater or a slanderer, a drunkard or a swindler. With such a man do not even eat. What business is it of mine to judge those outside the church? Are you not to judge those inside? God will judge those outside."

How far had I strayed from this attitude? How had I missed it?

Most Christians I know do much the opposite of this admonition. We don't associate with immoral people in the world and think ourselves better for it. We have tried to do what Paul apparently thought of as ridiculous—we've tried to leave the world in order to avoid these people. Don't we judge those outside the church by tacitly avoiding them, while constantly letting our own sins go unnoticed? Doesn't that amount to a twisting of this scripture?

God loves the world so much that He sent His Son to die for us all, that the world through Him might be saved. He came not to condemn the world, but to save it. Jesus did not insist that sinners take a moral bath before He would associate with them. Jesus moved around freely in the world because He loved people—all people. The only ones He didn't enjoy being around were the ones who thought their righteousness put them in a separate camp.

The apostle Paul also referred to people as those who were "being saved, and those who are perishing" (2 Corinthians 2:15). This is a way to look at people without spiritual pride or prejudice. To say a person is definitively a Christian or a non-Christian seems to make me or my group the judge. It closes the book on the case, and divides the sheep and the goats before they've been brought in. To say a person is *being saved* or is *perishing* leaves the book open and me out of the decision. It leaves me free to hope that, however rotten a person may appear to me, they may be, underneath their own wrestling, a person who is in the process of being saved.

There were two thieves on either side of Jesus when He died. Their lives brought them, seemingly, to a similar conclusion, and yet their last breaths showed that all along, there was a fundamental difference between them; one was being saved, and one was perishing. Who would have known? Who could have given a correct opinion concerning the destiny of these two desperate lives at any moment before that last gasp of breath? Certainly no one but the Man in the middle.

I must admit, I've gotten a head start on helping Jesus— the only Man in the middle—to separate the sheep from the goats. Next to male and female, whether a person is a Christian or a non-Christian has been a major consideration through most of my Christian experience. It determines whether they are "in" or "out," whether it is "us" or "them," whether I can speak in "Christianese" or I have to think of other words that mean what I want to say, whether I'm comfortable or uncomfortable with anyone.

How is it that most of us forget that once the tie has been broken between us and the rest of humanity there is no longer any real grounds for compassion or evangelism? If we are to go meet Christ where He died "outside the camp," then we must realize the group of people we are meeting there. These are the outsiders, the ones who know they need help and also the ones who may not know it yet. I am now discovering that there have been *lots* of things I have needed help with all these years; I've been one of the "us" Christians for a long time. What a joy it is to have finally discovered the fact that I am also one of "them." That is a liberating discovery!

I am proud to be among this group of needy people. I am overjoyed to be called to this Banquet of Grace. And I am thoroughly delighted not to have to decide who is going to be there and who is not—only to issue the invitation to everyone, and to gladly take my place *as one of them*, who has been invited and has decided to respond.

Based on these things, therefore, I have concluded that since I do not know the end of the story or the state of the heart, I am free to hope that everyone I meet could possibly be one who is being saved. Thus I will treat every person not as an enemy but as a friend; not as an outsider, but as one of "us" for whom Christ died.

When I think this way, I am no longer prejudiced or intimidated by the thought of spending a weekend with two non-Christian men.

But there was still the matter of relating to each other as *men*; forget my spiritual wrestlings.

It occurred to me that these two men were undoubtedly

as uneasy about this weekend proposal as I was. Disquiet-ing questions flooded my mind each time I began to do anything about setting up a first meeting. *What on earth are we doing this for? Everything is going along just fine with my life—why do I need this? I'm a normal American male—lonely, virtually friendless, covering my insecurities with a cloak of ad-equacy. Why shouldn't I be terrified about spending a weekend with two guys I hardly know? If I'm thinking these things, I can be sure they're thinking the same things too!*

I decided to take a creative approach that might disarm them. Go for the throat. Thus my first FAX message was born:

MEMO TO: JOHN WILLIAMS
                PHILLIP LUNT
FROM: JOHN FISCHER

AT A RECENT GATHERING OF NEIGHBORS IN MY ABSENCE, A DISCUSSION WITH MY WIFE RE-VEALED THE DESIRE TO PURSUE A CLOSER RE-LATIONSHIP BETWEEN THE THREE OF US MEN.

PLEASE MEET ME AT TEN CENTER STREET PUB ON THURSDAY, JANUARY 25, 7:00 P.M. TO DISCUSS FURTHER.

BRING YOUR CALENDARS AND YOUR SENSE OF ADVENTURE. I'LL BE THERE IF I DARE. . . .

I sent a copy to each of their places of work.

FAX #1 got an immediate response from Phillip. He could not recall the aforementioned conversation, but my FAX had definitely peaked his interest. I explained that I didn't know what was going on either, but if he could come on Thursday night, I was sure we'd all figure out some-thing. He then informed me he had a prior engagement and could not attend, but was interested in being included in what might become of this. I said I'd be happy to do that. Unfortunately, to his later chagrin, he didn't warn me about using the FAX machine anymore for such messages.

I thought about calling John, but I had already decided to show up for whoever did or didn't come.

At 5:00 P.M. on Thursday, John Williams called me:

John W: I'll be there.

John F: Great!

John W: Uh oh, did I just blow the mystery?

John F: That's okay. We'll just forget we ever had this conversation.

John W: OK. *Maybe* I'll be there.

John F: Yeah. Maybe I'll be there too. See you later.

He was already seated when I arrived, and we ended up talking for about an hour and a half about male insecurities, shallow relationships and spiritual hungers. We concluded we were up for spending at least an overnight together, even if it turned out to be just the two of us.

My next FAX message pretty much insured that:

MEMO TO: PHILLIP LUNT
FROM: JOHN FISCHER
JOHN WILLIAMS

THE MEETING OF THE THREE DID HAPPEN LAST NIGHT, REGRETFULLY WITHOUT YOUR IMPORTANT INPUT. HOWEVER, WE DID GO AHEAD WITH SOME CONCLUSIONS:

1) WE ARE LONELY, INSECURE, AND FRIGHTENED ABOUT ANYTHING BEYOND A CASUAL OR A BUSINESS RELATIONSHIP.
2) WE WANT TO DO SOMETHING ABOUT THIS.
3) GIVEN THAT THE THREE OF US ARE A HIGHLY UNLIKELY TRIO TO EVER GET TOGETHER FOR ANY OTHER REASON, IT SEEMED A PERFECT PLACE TO START.
4) THOUGH JOHN AND I HARDLY KNOW EACH OTHER, WE BOTH SHARE A DESIRE TO GET TO KNOW YOU BETTER.
5) WE NEED AT LEAST AN OVERNIGHT TO ESCAPE OBLIGATIONS AND BREAK DOWN DEFENSES, SO WE LOOKED AT WEEKENDS. FEBRUARY 9, 10 AND 23, 24 ARE GOOD FOR US AT THIS POINT.
6) WHAT WILL WE DO? JOHN W. HAS A TAPE OF

A POET AND SPEAKER WHO DOES MEN'S SEM-
INARS WHICH SOUNDED LIKE AN EXCELLENT
CATALYST FOR TALK. THE REST IS UP FOR
GRABS, EXCEPT WE DID AGREE ON SOME
GROUND RULES:
    1. NO TALKING ABOUT BUSINESS
    2. NO DRUGS
    3. NO EXPECTATIONS
7) LOCATION: YET TO BE DETERMINED. CABIN?
BOAT? HOTEL? A BAG UNDER THE STARS BY
FIRELIGHT? WHAT DO YOU THINK?
8) IF YOU'RE GAME, WE'D VERY MUCH LIKE YOU
TO BE A PART OF THIS ADVENTURE. NO
DOUBT WE'LL ALL BE TOO INVOLVED WITH
OTHER THINGS TO TALK MUCH ABOUT THIS
SATURDAY NIGHT AT THE PARTY AT YOUR
PLACE, BUT MAYBE THUMBS DOWN, OR
THUMBS UP AND A DATE WOULD BE APPRO-
PRIATE.

I sent the FAX on Friday. On Saturday night, John was
the first to broach the subject at the party at Phillip's house.

"Did you send a second FAX to my office yesterday?"
he asked.

"No."

He seemed relieved.

"Why? What's wrong?" I pursued.

"Obviously you haven't talked to Phillip yet. What did
you say in that thing, anyway?"

"Oh no," I said, beginning to get the picture. Phillip,
fortunately, was in the next room programming the stereo.
"What happened?"

"Apparently it created quite a stir in his office. Something about 'no drugs,' and 'sleeping bags under the
stars . . .' "

"Is he laughing about it yet?" I asked, looking for a place
to hide.

"I think he's okay now. It wouldn't have been so bad if
there hadn't been a team of new clients from England

standing around the FAX machine waiting for an important message from the home office at the moment it came through. They read every word."

"Oh no!"

"You better talk to him."

Later in the evening when Phillip was finally alone, I snuck up behind him and chanced an announcement: "Rule number four: No more FAX messages!"

He was indeed laughing about it, at least I think he was laughing, but he was also understandably skittish about any further exploits of the unlikely three musketeers.

Chapter Ten
Friends Anonymous

SNOW SEASON HAS LONG been upon us now. Six inches fell last night without making a sound. Though the build-up continued well into the middle of this morning, I decided not to wait for it to stop before clearing the driveway. I'm not equipped to handle much more than six inches at a time. As it turned out, the sun was breaking through by the time I was done. Few sights I know are more glorious than this: bright sunshine on the new-fallen snow that hugs our New England house.

Like mowing the lawn in summer and raking the leaves in the fall, shoveling the snow in winter is something I am deeply dedicated to doing *myself*. Marti doesn't understand why I am so religious about it. She thinks we should hire someone to do jobs like this and get on with more important things. She doesn't realize that when I'm out in the cold air, feeling the heat of my body beneath a flannel shirt and a coat, hearing the shovel-scrape swallowed up by a white blanket, and anticipating the reward of a hot cup of coffee inside, knowing my house is snug and easily accessible—she doesn't realize that, at the moment, there is simply nothing more important in the world to me than this.

At least on a day like today, when there's time for this—when no one has to get anywhere, and the sun is out. There have been other days when this shoveling thing has not been so romantic—days when I have had to chop away the ice that builds up and blocks the swinging garage doors, when the snow was wet and heavy and pulled muscles in my back and neck, when the wind was raw and my fingers went numb, when I just cleared the whole driveway and a few hours later had to do it all over again because of a fresh fall. Yes, time chips away at the novelty of this. There are times when I see the wisdom of my wife's suggestion and envy Chuck who hasn't even cleared his driveway yet today because he has a snowplow on his pick-up and he'll take care of it in a matter of minutes sometime this afternoon from the warmth of his cab.

But this morning was one of those exceptional mornings. I will remember it for a long time: sun breaking through on crisp white; the heaviness of a clouded winter sky, broken.

There were other stalwart shovelers out, being that it was a Saturday. I felt only a distant kinship with them as we exchanged silent waves of mittened hands—the two teenaged sons of the neighbor on the other side of Malcolm's house, and the pastor of the local parish who lives on the far corner of the Green (now the "White"). Seeing their forms, dark on white as their breath made frozen puffs in the air, and feeling the insulation of the snow—all of it made me sense again my aloneness here.

In the weeks since we first talked, nothing has happened between John and me. We haven't gotten together yet, and Phillip has made it clear he's not interested in pursuing this idea any further. Phillip comes as no surprise, but the part about John and me is unsettling. In spite of the fact that we could have pulled this thing off, calendar pages have flipped by and we haven't. It's not that we don't both want this, we are simply avoiding it.

How odd it is. These guys are major businessmen who manage large accounts and constantly keep themselves out on the creative edge of their work. I put myself out in front of hundreds of people on a regular basis. And yet, when faced with putting ourselves out in front of each other in a vulnerable way, well, let's just say our schedules suddenly get real full.

Why is it so hard for men to open up to each other? So many grunts, so many jokes, so many slaps on the back—so much pride and competition. I notice, when I'm in the company of men, I'm constantly measuring myself and usually coming up short in my own mind, but covering up that insecurity in one way or another.

It's as if we're afraid someone will find out who we really are. As if we didn't already know. We all know—or at least we have a pretty good idea—that everyone else is just as insecure as we are, but we all seem to have this unspoken agreement not to let it out of the bag and break the code of secrecy.

I think that's what went "wrong" with John and me. We broke the code. The FAX that I so indiscreetly exposed to all those British businessmen in Phillip's office broke the code in front of them all. Though we never did follow through with our meetings, I suppose we did at least accomplish this. I must admit, it felt good to be face-to-face with John—someone I barely knew, who was not a Christian, but could at least admit he had deep unmet needs like mine, someone who was not pretending to be strong and have it all together for fear that someone else might put him down.

When Jacob and Esau finally had a reunion they wept, kissed each other, and then settled a long distance apart. This is typical male behavior. A kind of awkward stab at closeness—followed by a retreat to an even greater distance. Not geographical distance, but a deeper isolation increased by the knowledge of briefly touching and then rejecting what could have been.

So John and I "kissed" and settled a distance apart.

There is one male friend, however, with whom I can be honest and not feel threatened. He's a friend sometimes I wish I could hide from. He walks around in an unkempt manner, with a permanent contortion on his face due to a chronically analytical mind: His sins and addictions surround him like a personal cloud.

This friend represents, in many ways, all the hidden unpleasantness in my own character. We both grew up in strongly Christian homes, except that he was subjected to a legalistic Christian environment of cultic proportions that mentally abused him as a child. Like me, he sought identity in his art form, but unlike me, he retreated into his art so deeply that he rejected normal human relationships and became socially inept. His sins are obvious, and perhaps this is what makes our relationship possible. He is too sick to try and fool anybody about himself, and I am finally smart enough not to try and fool anybody, either.

Of all the cool people I've known over the years—the popular and the famous—this man is my one *true* male friend. There is no play acting between us: it's laughed away before even attempted. There are no requirements and no expectations other than to be real, and that is not a pressure point. It will simply be obvious if either one of us tries to cover.

I struggle with this relationship at times. I'm scared by it for the opposite reason I would be scared about a weekend with John or Phillip. With them, I'd be intimidated by the unknown; with this friend I'm intimidated by the *known*. There's no place to run or to hide. And yet, what makes this relationship so wonderful, in spite of its unlikely existence, is our shared life in Christ. There is always an abundance of love and acceptance here.

This relationship would not have become what it is, were it not for our shared isolation in New England. I know I wouldn't have had a relationship like this in California— there would have been too many other, more desirable friendships to choose from. I would be the poorer for it, for they would have been the kind of relationships that tolerated a certain distance. They would have been safe, and less than totally accepting. We would all have acted so healthy around each other. This relationship is accepting and dangerous, but out here in winter, where most bodies will give you no more than a mittened wave across the cold whiteness, if you once grab hold of a warm hand you learn to hold on tight.

I keep getting up to check the window when the dogs bark; not the side window with the bare tree, but the one toward the front of the house. I'm half-expecting my friend to show up this evening. The snow that fell last weekend is now all dented and scarred by children's boot-prints, shoveled leaves, road dirt, and the frozen duties of neighborhood dogs.

My friend has admitted he may be an alcoholic and just this week attended his first A.A. meeting. He works nights and stops by here often when he needs a cup of coffee and some company instead of a fifth of something stronger. This is a safe place for him, and I'm happy to provide it. But I also resent being pulled away from my work. I told him that next time he went to an A.A. meeting I wanted to go with him. I'd like to find out what it feels like being in a room full of people who all publicly acknowledge they have something wrong with them.

I've spent nearly all my life being around people who publicly acknowledge they *used to* have something wrong with them. ("Of course there are still a few things here and there that need some work. But then again, we're in process, you know. 'God isn't finished with me yet.' ") It used to feel good to be around "together" people—it made me feel everything was going pretty well with me, thank you. I remember, when I was "healthy," how we used to deal with those who were weak, addicted, unable to manage their lives. We called them a "drain," because we would keep pouring in truth and their broken situation would go on and on, perpetuating itself. I always wondered why what was working for us didn't seem to work for them. Never once did it occur to me to question whether there might be something wrong with us—something wrong with the whole system by which we judged ourselves as "better." Were we really "better," or were we merely on the side that got to make the standard of judgment? Were we "better" because of the truth, or because we got to decide what "better" was? My friend here would have been a "drain" in that system. Who was sick? Who was really getting healthy?

I used to think he was a drain on me. That's no longer the case. I may view him as a distraction or an embarrassment, but that's only when I'm unwilling to look at myself, for being with him almost always reveals the truth about me in some way. And in spite of the distance he has to go in working out his own salvation, he almost always gives me a fresh perspective on where I am in working out mine.

Having spent so much time around people who had nothing wrong with them, I feel it would be a great relief to be around people who knew they were in trouble on a daily basis, so much so that they had no room at all for judging anyone else. Imagine being in a room and not worrying about being judged by anyone. Imagine being in a *church* and not worrying about being judged by anyone.

There's another reason I'd like to go with my friend to an A.A. meeting. I'm beginning to get the point about Jesus dying for outsiders. What does Hebrews mean when it says we should "meet Him outside the camp, bearing the disgrace He bore"? What does that mean especially to someone like me who's been on the inside for so long? I don't think I know; I haven't been in many places that are very disgraceful. Most of the places I've been in are honored places—spiritually honored. But an A.A. meeting would be a place where disgrace goes public.

The phone rings and I pick up the receiver. It's my friend saying he's headed for a meeting in ten minutes and do I want to come. He also tells me he checked the book and these are supposed to be closed meetings—alcoholics only.

I wonder if I could qualify. Certainly I'm addicted to escapism, which makes my life unmanageable periodically. As I've admitted, I can go into mental lock-out when facing a financial crisis, unable to perform the simplest tasks. I excuse myself from doing anything about the problem due to the state I'm in. I think I know what it is to be addicted to "numbness," so as to escape fear and worry. I know what it is to have my mind whirl out of control with thoughts and plans and schemes to try and fix things—only to get bogged down in all the imaginary causes and effects of my various plans. I know what it is to try and pray, or read the Bible, when I'm in such a state, and to feel as if nothing is getting through. And I know what it's like to sit down over a cup of coffee with someone who loves me and can help me sort through the mess my mind has gotten in, someone who also knows the Lord and can remind me of His grace and mercy and sovereign control over my life and my future. . . . You know, I think I could qualify for this meeting.

Instead, I tell him I'm busy writing and to try me again next time. Then I hang up, feeling like someone who is trying to pin dead leaves back onto winter-cleaned branches. Why not get honest about my reasons for dodging this. . . .

It's my ego again. If I went to an A.A. meeting, everyone would think I was an alcoholic and how would *that* feel? Something tells me I need to find out.

Something tells me I need to honestly address a question I have not spoken out loud until now: I wonder if you can be addicted to God—if you can attach to God in an unhealthy way. I know it's hard to imagine that anything to do with God could be detrimental, but I think the thought bears some consideration. Obviously, it depends on whether you truly know God, or are merely using some supposed knowledge about Him as an escape, and a defense, much the way an alcoholic uses a drink. Addiction, in a spiritual sense, would mean that you *use* ideas about God and neat stories about God and scripture verses about God to drown your own failure, incompetence, and fear; in that sense, you could be . . . addicted to God. If this were the case, it would be worse to be addicted to God than to be an alcoholic. An alcoholic can go to God for help; a person addicted to God stuff would be self-deceived into thinking they've already had their help. It would be like having a light within you that was darkness; like thinking you can see when you are blind. Jesus warned about this in Matthew 5, and He must have seen it being done or He wouldn't have brought it up. As a matter of fact, I think I've done it.

Of course, you wouldn't be addicted to the real presence of God, only to your own ideas about Him. A real relation-ship with God, just like a membership in A.A., requires a daily admission of powerlessness and need. Such a person doesn't "use" God. They don't have enough control over their life for that. A person who is addicted to God, then, would be one who never stops talking about God, is never caught without the right answer or the right verse to quote. But in the midst of all this so-called spirituality is a very insecure, guilt-ridden, manipulating, twisted, frightened individual. For this kind of person to admit these faults, acknowledge their manipulation of God and spiritual things for their own advantage, and to admit their pow-erlessness before God—whoever He is, for He would have to be reconstructed from all their wrong ideas about Him—would be the first step on the road to recovery. Such a person, if they wanted to recover, would probably find a lot to identify with at an A.A. meeting.

The basic issue seems to be control. Who's in control here? Is God in control of us, or are we in control of our ideas about Him? Perhaps this is part of what it means to go "outside the camp"—to bear the disgrace He bore. Jesus was dragged outside the city walls and crucified. This was the procedure for common criminals—murderers, thieves, political revolutionaries, thugs, addicts, alcoholics. This was the company Jesus kept in death. It was also part of the procedure of sin sacrifice for the Jewish high priest. The blood of the animal was offered in the Holy Place, but the body was taken outside the camp and burned. "And so Jesus also suffered outside the city gate to make the people holy . . . Let us, then, go to Him outside the camp. . . ." The blood that makes us holy is in the holy place—*but where are we supposed to be?*

Outside. Outside the camp. Outside the city gate. Outside the inner circle. "For here we do not have an enduring city, but we are looking for the city that is to come" (Hebrews 13:12–14).

The minute I think I'm "in" somewhere is the time to start looking for a way out, because this isn't it. If I've gotten myself into a pretty good place with pretty good people, then I shouldn't expect it to last very long. If I think there's no place for me at an A.A. meeting, then I'd better think again. There's no lasting place here. There's no holy of holies where we can comfortably commune until the Lord comes back. There's no city here. No running water. No sewage control. No transportation. NO CITY!

No, we meet the Lord outside the city where we take Him our sin daily—our real sin, our "solid sin" as Oswald Chambers puts it in *My Utmost for His Highest*. "What our Lord wants us to present to Him is not goodness, nor honesty, nor endeavor, but real solid sin; that is all He can take from us. And what does He give us in exchange for our sin? Real solid righteousness. But we must relinquish all pretense of being anything, all claim of being worthy of God's consideration."

Christian fellowship, unfortunately, deals mostly with the airy stuff. The point, of course, is that there are no grades of sin. Sin is sin; it's just that we tend to look at it differently, depending on where we are and who we're with. . . .

I pick up the receiver to call my friend back and catch him just as he's going out the door. "Stop by and pick me up. I want to go with you after all."

Thus it was that Wednesday morning, 10:00 A.M., found me crammed into a room at Anna Jacques Hospital, with more than fifty male members of the Newburyport chapter of Alcoholics Anonymous. They spanned all ages and every social level. They looked, for the most part, very ordinary. It could have just as easily been a men's retreat from the First Baptist Church.

The first fifteen minutes were taken up with announcements. They were done with humor, and a few of the more regular members were "poked" at in good-natured fun. Most of the men laughed, and I felt a strange familiarity with them. Then the main speaker talked for about forty-five minutes about his life and what A.A. , the men in A.A. , and God had done for him. The first thing I noticed was that he didn't stand up to speak. No one did all morning. I don't know if it's an unwritten rule, but the impression it gave me was that none of these guys considered themselves more special than anyone else there.

His talk was a testimonial. He was a heavy-set man in his late fifties, with a round face somewhat shaded by a green tennis hat that he wore the whole morning. He sat behind a table with two apparent leaders of the group and talked about his history of addiction, denial and salvation. He talked about how his life was now stabilized in a relatively good balance, and how he has actually begun to enjoy living for the first time.

It was surprising to me to find how large a role God played in his life, and how easy it was for him to talk about Him. His most memorable encounters with God centered around sober experiences in nature—the autumn foliage in Vermont or a sunrise in Maine. He spoke of miraculous timings of phone calls and brushes with accountability that he was hardpressed to explain apart from divine intervention. He said, though he was an ardent non-believer when he started in A.A. , he had come to see there was no way out of his addiction apart from help from a Higher Power. His earthy apologetic was this: "I'd rather live my life believing there is a God, than to live it thinking there's *no* God and find out I was wrong." It met with a chorus of under-standing Esau-like grunts in the room—a sort of non-religious "Amen."

When he talked of God, he was careful not to push his beliefs on anyone. You didn't have to believe in God to come to A.A. , the most important thing was that you kept coming. No one was going to make you do anything you didn't want to do. These men were all respected for their own choices, be they good or bad. The most important part was facing the bad choices, facing what they had done to your life, and deciding whether or not you wanted help in making better choices. If you want help, then keep coming, get a sponsor—someone you can call whenever you think you have to have a drink—and keep coming back, every day if necessary.

When he finished, there was loud applause. Then everyone squeezed out of two side doors for a break. One door went to a dingy smoke-filled employee dining room, the other went outside. Since it was an unseasonably pleasant day, and my friend wanted a cigarette, we decided to take in some fresh air.

As we stepped around patches of melting snow, I reflected quietly on the strange movements of God that brought me here where my best Christian friend is a chain-smoking alcoholic and my worst non-Christian friends are non-smoking, successful businessmen. Things are not always what they appear to be.

We returned to a half-hour of hearing similar testimonials from the group. Each one began with: "I'm George, and I'm an alcoholic," or "I'm Norm, and I'm a drunk." The room would echo immediately and boisterously, "Hi, George," or "Hi, Norm." What followed was an account of their struggle with addiction. When they were through—regardless of whether they were on the up-side or the down-side of that struggle—there would be another echo in the room, "Thanks, George," or "Thanks, Norm."

Then, at precisely 11:30, as if on cue, everyone stood up, and these fifty irresolute men held hands and together recited the Lord's prayer. The only change was "and give us this day our daily *strength*"—which was to say what bread does for you; and these men needed to hear it in that more simplified way, depending, as they were, on a source of power greater than themselves to keep them from depending on anything else.

I too needed to hear about daily real dependence in this way, to see my struggles with sin as no different than theirs. I suddenly felt no more special than any of the guys there, but strangely special along with them—more special than I'd ever felt before. It was a specialness attached only to the grace of God: It felt clean and honest. I need God for the same reason they need Him. As we walked out to the parking lot, I couldn't help remarking, "Well, I don't know about you, but that felt like church."

I've been doing a lot of thinking, since Wednesday's meeting, about Cain and Abel. They both brought offerings to God from the fruit of their hands. Abel, who was a shepherd, brought a lamb. Cain, a farmer, brought forth produce from the fields. There's no indication from the scriptural account that God told them ahead of time what to bring. It appears simply that Abel happened to be in the right profession for sacred offerings to Yahweh.

It's understandable that Cain got upset that Abel's offering was accepted and his was not. His mistake was that he thought *he* was being rejected, when it was only his offering that was unacceptable. Finding this out, he could easily have traded some corn for one of Abel's lambs and brought an acceptable offering. Instead, out of anger, envy, and a mistaken sense of his own rejection, he killed his brother. Cain is most often the one we think about in this story; Abel is always written off as the poor victim. But I wonder—what about Abel? Could he have made the opposite mistake? Could he have assumed that since his offering was accepted, he was somehow better than Cain? Could he, like Cain, have confused himself with the offering and concluded that he was more acceptable to God than his brother? If he did, then he would also have been guilty, and my sin would be like unto the sin of Abel.

I have brought proper offering to God from childhood. I have done the right thing from the beginning. I was born into this. I got it right the first time just because I happened to be in the right place, born into the right family. I was prayed over, encouraged, loved and led to the altar before I even knew what I was doing. Abel and I got lucky. The assumption was wrong. The assumption was: because of these blessings, I am somehow better than other people. I was dead wrong.

Just now I found myself feeling only a little bit scared in a room full of Cains, and finally I think I've got it. I'm no different from these guys. Just because I happened to get the offering right in the first place doesn't mean I'm any less in need of it, or any more acceptable in God's eyes. The offering is Jesus Christ, the lamb of God, and we're all acceptable only on the basis of what He's done. That's why it had to be a lamb.

Nobody is better than anyone else—we've just got to make sure we get the offering right.

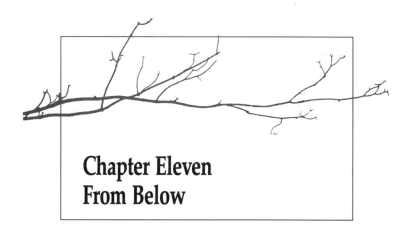

Chapter Eleven
From Below

THIS MORNING, as I stare out once again at the rugged maple tree, with no more leaves to hide behind, I am thinking about the parts of the tree I can't see. It is one thing to hit bottom, learn some things, and bounce back; it's another thing to live there.

I know two people who live on the bedrock reality of life all the time—two women who have dug deeply into my life. One is a loyal friend; the other, who is not willing to stay even at the level of friendship with me, is my wife and lover. Together they make up my understanding of woman. I could call them Leah and Rachel, I could call them, simply, Woman, but their real names are Kathy and Marti.

When my branches were green and spreading in California, Kathy was there. By odd happenstance, she too now lives in New England, so she has watched me and known me from a distance through many seasons. I had no way of knowing how important this relationship would become.

I remember her from California days only as a very cognizant person, with curled eyebrows and sharp eyes. She sat in the first Bible study I ever taught, and wouldn't accept shoddy thinking. Even then, though I hardly ever spoke with her, I can remember feeling uncomfortable with her, as if she knew something about me she wasn't telling. Her eyes always made me feel bare and vulnerable. I have since realized that was more my own feeling than a function she consciously performed: It's my own sense that I'm not telling the whole truth about myself that her rootedness always brings out in me.

It has taken the vulnerable nature of winter to discover my need for such a rooted person. She has become to me the awakener of my vision, the rattler of my conscience, the fire-builder in my heart—a lover of my soul. Kathy is my wife's best friend and my soul-mate, and she asks for nothing in return.

Some would say all of this deeper relationship should come from one source, my wife. But who would place such a heavy demand on any one person? I have no more interest in sharing the marriage bed with a discerning "sword" than my wife has in wielding one there. Besides, Marti has her own male friendships where she has no problem bringing out the sword of honesty. They come for this, much as I might ask the same thing of Kathy.

I've heard a lot about mates who are both friends and lovers for each other. I've heard most of the songs on this subject. I know of marriages where this works, but my wife has requested otherwise. She wants to be other than my friend, she wants to be my lover. She welcomes Kathy as both her friend and mine. If relationships like this are rare, then we are blessed.

This friend and soul-mate has been long accustomed to viewing life from the underside. A childhood accident tore half of Kathy's face away, and the experience so scarred her emotionally that to this day, whenever she looks into a mirror, she does not see a face. Her skin is translucent, and the scar begins near her eye and disappears into the hair of her forehead. She has seen so many sides of life, and has been so close to death, that when you look in her face you are looking into a mirror of more than you want to see. It's as if, for Kathy, superficial reality was torn away when she lost her face, leaving it impossible for her to ever deal with people on appearances alone. Around Kathy, you see what has been torn open, and you fear somehow that you may be exposed, as well.

Kathy's discernment, like all spiritual gifts that are used in love, is only given on a supply and demand basis. I have asked much of this gift, and am free to ask of it at any time. I always receive an answer—and though I may not want to hear it, it will always be true. That look on her face that I once confused with divine foreknowledge, I know now, was only her familiarity with life's dirt. Perhaps it was an unconscious fear that if she got too close to my face, she might grab it and peel it away too, revealing the true nature of my mind and heart.

This closeness to bedrock reality is something I have come to know as present in these two women. Kathy and Marti live three feet *below* the ground. Their souls reach deep into life's earth and bring forth nourishment, that buds might sprout and birds might nest high in the branches. Their task is always the same, and should the tree for some reason be cut down, it would remain the same, and they would continue bringing up nutrients for nothing. Like all women, their perspective is always from underneath. They never rise above you, but see you as Mary saw Christ on the cross. From below and dying. Life, for them, appears to be seasonless; the ground is the same all year long, only a little colder near the surface in winter.

I used to not think this way. I used to think men had their feet in the ground while women were floating off-center in the air. Then Marti became pregnant with our first child, and my wife, the supposedly emotional and flighty one, was aware of everything that was going on—every presence in the room, every tick of the clock, every on-slaught of pain—and when our child came forth from her substance, she was the first to grab its wet messy body and hold it close to her chest. And me? I was hovering somewhere in the room in emotional disarray. Even our memories bear this out. Hers are precise; mine are a blur.

This frazzled-father image has traditionally been attributed to a helpless, detached state of mind. The baby, at home for nine months in its mother's womb, is, to a man, a mysterious alien body. I don't believe this explanation goes deep enough. Not when you add the memory of our second child who came two months early while we were away from home, and my wife, standing in the hotel room with blood and water running down her legs, calmly instructed me as to the steps I should take in getting us to the hospital. No, there's more to this than the frazzled-father story.

Why is it that, in spite of her decidedly feminine nature and elegant dress, Marti is always the first to plunge her hands into the finger-paints, join in a water fight, or roll on the floor with the children? In fact, she has always been more comfortable on the floor than in a chair.

Why is it that when I work in the yard, I walk about handsomely raking, trimming and riding the mower, while when Marti works in the yard, rare as that may be, she lunges into the flower bed, all knees and mud and elbows?

Why is it that she is always the one to bring up plans for the future—retirement, health insurance, college education for the children, vacation, investments? When she does this, I feel as if my mind is being pulled from a notion somewhere in the clouds, to an uncomfortable fact somewhere in the real world.

Why is it that Kathy, whenever called upon, will stop what she is doing and immediately enter into whatever confusion or uncertainty I am bringing to her and help me reduce it to its basic common denominator? Why is it that she can so easily recall to me the simple, basic truth about Jesus that I can complicate so in living?

I've since decided to reconstruct this whole image. It's the women in my life who are grounded, stable, rooted in the earth; I'm the one who shimmers on the branch, skittish as a bird. I deal mostly with thoughts, ideas, and concepts. The women I know, though they can hold their own with male thoughts, ideas and concepts, tend to deal more directly with survival, blood and pain. How often is my head lost in the cloud of spiritual realities, while their hands are in the dirt of human experience. They are more likely to have gut-level reactions; I am more calculating, but sometimes frozen in the mental process of those calculations. I notice, for instance, that I can distance myself from the human drama, while Marti almost always remains engaged. Our daughter gets injured and she is immediately swept up in Marti's arms, or a friend stops by, distraught, and Marti stops what she's doing and gives her undivided attention. I, on the other hand, try to figure out how to avoid interruptions and get on with my original plan for the day. I want to fulfill the vision for this day.

> Your old men will dream dreams,
> Your young men will see visions.
> Joel 2:28

I truly believe there is something to men dreaming dreams and having visions and women birthing those dreams and visions into reality. These perspectives have certainly been borne out in my observation. This is what we bring to each other. I've never picked Marti up off the ground when it didn't light up her face. It may be only two feet off the living room floor, but for her, the important thing is, for a moment *she is off the ground*. She, on the other hand, is always pulling me down to earth—trying to get me to connect with the immediate issues around us—to get rooted into reality.

Marti has always wanted to fly. She was a flight attendant for nine years, and her unrealized dream was to be a pilot. To fly is to be released from an earthly hold—to see life from another perspective. I believe this is why Marti is always seeking romance from me. Romance lifts her away from the earth. It allows her to dream, to fly. It appears to me to be a forgone conclusion: women seek romance; men seek sex. This is not hard to understand. Women want to be released from their rootedness; men want to root themselves somewhere. This is why in a marriage, sex without romance is a form of abuse. The man gets what he wants; the woman doesn't.

A church, a marriage, or a society that diminishes the value of a woman's viewpoint will be severely lacking in its connection to anything rooted in the real world. Women are the "so what?" of life. I can be in the presence of God for days, fast and pray, and come down from the mountain, as it were, with my face still aglow, but if the truths I bring from this high and lofty place fail in their ability to be interpreted into life by the women around me, they might as well have been left there. They will be of no use to anyone's real experience.

Last Christmas, I attended a presentation by a Christian college choir in a large southern California church. The whole evening had a relaxed informality about it—but it was an informality under the conscious control of the choral director, a kind of planned casualness that I recognize now as typical of southern California lifestyle. The female students in the choir had all punched themselves out of the same cardboard cut-out book. They all must have gone to the same hair dresser. They were all perfect.

At one point in the evening, the president of the college was introduced, and one of the male students in the choir introduced the president's wife as "the First Lady of the College." The First Lady stood, revolved, and sat down. She looked like a person who had a lot to say if given the chance, but only her husband spoke. The only woman who did speak was the choir director's wife, and she quoted, from memory, various Christmas passages from the *New Testament*. She—bearer of life herself, swaddler of her own flesh and blood, laborer in her own pains, entertainer of shepherds—was given a part to memorize and recite on the celebration of a human birth, an event on which she is the expert. She did the best she could—faltering at times in her memory, but soft and sweet and charming in her delivery. Someone gave her this part. She never would have faltered had she spoken as a true Mary, acquainted as she was with the visitation of men wiser than these, and still following the star. I looked around at the faces of those charmed by the sweet voice, and realized they too had the same hairdresser. It was all so perfect.

I wanted to stand up and scream.

Men will forever be comfortable with mothers they can complain about, beauty queens they can adore from a distance, and Barbie dolls they can dress and undress. But give us a brilliant mind, or a scarred face that mirrors our sin and pulls us down into the roots of life, and we will prefer to give her a script instead. It is a fearful thing to become vulnerable to reality. I'm sad for the women who have accepted the script, and denied their own nature in an attempt to live out the myths that men place on them.

Hey guys, remember my inner room—the one where I marked my Bible with the precise point of a pen? I have an idea. Let's get a bunch of men together, go back in there and see what we can come up with. I'm sure we could get our heads together and agree upon our own idea of reality, a much safer one than this one we've got now. And I bet, without too much effort, we could probably compose a theology that would have us convinced that, had Eve offered us the fruit, we most certainly would have refused it.

On the contrary, however, I have eaten the fruit, and I would do it again. I would be drawn into this knowledge of good and evil, however painful—however disastrous the consequences for myself or my offspring—rather than to remain disconnected, innocent, aloof. I would be brought down, for if I have failed to protect Eve from the beguilement of Satan, I will not fail a second time by refusing to join her in this oneness, and know what it is that I have done. I would not choose to remain in a garden, however Edenic, from which she alone had been banished.

It's time to get busy recovering what I've lost—instead of wasting time standing around with the guys, nursing my fragile ego and blaming someone else for this juice that still sticks to my chin.

Chapter Twelve
A Tree Like No Other

THE ONLY EDIBLE PART of our maple tree also leaves behind sticky chins—sticky knives and forks and breakfast tables too. It is one of nature's rarities in that the "fruit" of a maple tree is found only in late winter.

There has just been a period of freezing, followed by a period of thawing. This is when New England weather can move the mercury drastically in any direction. This is when the outer edges of the tree begin to call the sap back again. Sweet goodness rises from within, in a slow but powerful movement.

This is a by-product of the maple that cannot simply be plucked from its branches like an apple or an orange. It must be drawn from within, from deep inside its trunk. The sweetwater "sap" of the maple tree from which syrup is made is different from the circulatory sap of the growing season. Malcolm told me that. Drawing on it will not lessen the tree's life-flow or deplete its strength for the coming spring.

For commercial purposes, a tap hole is bored through the tree's crusty outer bark, and the liquid seeps out into buckets, or it's fed through plastic lines to where it can be processed. But the same sap will flow from any wound on the tree. Like the sweetwater life that flowed from the side of Christ, the blood and water of our redemption, there is a sweetness that can flow from the wounds life gives to us, as well.

This sweetness flows by our faith—by living in deep-down union with Christ. It seeps its way out through the cuts and gashes and losses inflicted upon us. It pours out through the lips of the wound itself, allowing others to taste its sweetness. Were it not for the tree's wounds, or the steel tap driven into its side, this sweetwater sap would stay inside and never be shared. This sweetness is known only to those who draw it out during the first thaws of winter.

I can sense a seven-year thaw coming on. Reflecting, praying—looking for the deeper meaning in beliefs I once held so superficially—this is what is drawing life from the depths of me, out toward the surface again. So much work, to arrive at simple but true life. It takes thirty to fifty gallons of sap to yield one gallon of maple syrup. That's a lot of processing. So our own beliefs must be processed through real life—through joy and sorrow both—before anyone else can benefit from their sweetness. "Make a practice of provoking your own mind to think out what it accepts easily. Our position is not ours until we make it ours by suffering," says Oswald Chambers.

One thing I have always accepted easily, yet never before thought out carefully, is self-denial. "If anyone would come after me, he must deny himself and take up his cross and follow me" (Matthew 16:24). What does it mean?

Did Jacob do this—and still wrestle with God? Did Marti do this while running the Fellowship of Christian Airline Personnel? Can Christians deny themselves without becoming "wimpy"?

I discovered recently how little I know about the true meaning of self-denial during a conversation with Marti. She has an outgoing personality, a natural ability to influence influential people, a sense of God's leading in her life, and has been very successful in leadership positions in public relations and public affairs. All of this has led us to believe that this is the type of vocation in which she belongs—building organizational platforms from which influential people can affect society in positive ways. This is not me.

On a personal level, our differences have always been the catalyst as well as the conundrum of our marriage. Marti sits on the edge of her chair; I lean back, casually. Marti desires—but is often denied—the spotlight; I shun it and get pushed out into it anyway. Marti seems destined to an influential place in the secular world; I am trying to be responsible with one in the Christian world.

In this case, however, Marti had been weakened by circumstances to the point where she was questioning our assumptions about her. She was wrestling with God as to whether He was asking her to deny her own personality as we had come to understand it.

"Maybe we've been wrong," she said. "Could God be asking me to deny what is intrinsically *me?*"

I replied with, "No, I don't believe God would ask you to deny yourself—to deny who you are." And then it caught me—the verse, the tape, the word hidden in my heart that in this case was about to explode in my face: "If any one would follow me, let him *deny himself.* . . ." *Oh dear*, I thought, *I've just contradicted Jesus.* And so, to make sure I was safe with the truth, and without thinking through at all what it might mean in Marti's situation, I spoke from somewhere in the clouds and said, "But Jesus did say we were to deny ourselves, take up our cross and follow Him. . . ."

"But what does that mean?" she pressed.

"Well, I'm not sure. . . ."

"Then don't give me the verse if you don't know what it means."

I felt as if God had pulled the pin and handed me the grenade—and I took one look at it and quickly passed it off to Marti and jumped into a foxhole.

I've heard this verse all my life, but when it came right down to a practical understanding of its truth in direct relationship to my wife, I couldn't draw the line between the verse and the reality. Did this verse have any implications for me? No doubt it did, but I certainly wasn't going to hang around long enough to find any. This is the *pass-it-off-and-jump-in-the-hole* style of scriptural counseling. It has more to do with protecting yourself in relation to what the scripture *might* mean than with taking responsibility to find out what it *does* mean in a given situation.

So the next morning, sufficiently rebuked, I got out my concordances and my dictionaries, firmly intent on getting to the bottom of this. What I found was indeed an explosion, but not at all the one I thought was coming. What I found was a key to getting rid of the weakness, wimpiness and disconnectedness that I am trying to uncover in my life and in the particular brand of Christianity I have lived with.

Now I'm no theologian, but here's what became clear to me.

With Webster's help, I came up with three basic definitions of the word *deny*:

1. *To declare not to be true; contradict.* . . . This could not be what Jesus is asking of us. He would not ask us to declare ourselves not to be true, or to contradict ourselves. In 2 Timothy 2:13, Paul is quoting a trustworthy saying when he writes, "If we are faithless he (God) will remain faithful, for he cannot *deny* himself." God would not ask us to do what He cannot do.

The denial spoken about here, the denial God would not do nor ask us to do, is the denial of one's own intrinsic self. God never denied, or contradicted himself. God did deny himself something when He humbled himself and took on the form of a servant (Philippians 2:5–8), but that was a denial of His *rights* as God, not a denial of His true nature as God.

When Paul says, "I have been crucified with Christ and it is no longer I who live but Christ lives in me, and the life I live in the body, I live by faith in the Son of God who loved me and gave himself for me" (Galatians 2:20), notice that the "I" stays throughout this statement. The "I" is Paul. It is who Paul is, intrinsically. It is what sets Paul apart from Jacob and Marti and me and God. God would never ask Paul to declare this *identity* to not be true. Though Paul has gone through a crucifixion, the "I" is still intact, and all of his letters indicate that at any time, he can make choices as to what the "I" is going to do.

2. *To refuse to grant, gratify, or yield to. . . .* This seems to me the closest thing to what Jesus meant. In the Greek lexicon it also gave the definition "to say no." To deny myself, therefore, means to refuse to grant myself my own wishes. To say "no" to myself. When I get up to work at 5 A.M. instead of sleeping, I am denying my natural desire to be lazy. I have grabbed the hair on the back of my neck and pulled myself into a work day. I may be half-groggy, my body wanting to go back to bed—but fulfilling responsibilities instead. This is the opposite of self-indulgence. It goes against all of the philosophies of the age: "go for it," "you deserve it," "pamper yourself," "indulge yourself." To not gratify or yield to myself means I must yield to another—namely, to God and to my neighbor, as well.

3. *To disclaim connection with or responsibility for. . . .* Neither can this be the kind of denial Jesus means, for He is always addressing our sense of responsibility. This is what Peter did to Jesus outside the high priest's courtyard. This is not what He asks us to do to ourselves. Disconnect ourselves from ourselves? How do you do that? Disclaim any responsibility for ourselves? Surely not.

And yet something dawned on me as I studied these definitions: the Christianity I am most familiar with has managed to get these definitions exactly backwards. To indulge myself, to grant myself my wishes, is twisted around until it is actually interpreted as a blessing from God to the one who has enough faith to claim it.

And there is also a *self-destructive* side to the Christianity I have learned, in which "to deny myself" means to disconnect from myself in some way. Instead of simply saying "no" to my selfish rights, I am taught to deny myself falsely: "Oh, I'm just a worm. I didn't achieve anything—it was God in me. I'm just a miserable bag of garbage saved by grace."

Recently, I was at a banquet, sitting next to a woman who launched into one of these speeches after she'd just been thanked publicly for some great effort. I surprised her *and* myself by blurting out, "No, it wasn't God—it was you! Sure He had a hand in it, but so did you. Don't deny what you did. It's very important."

We looked at each other and almost dropped our forks. We knew I was right, but it felt so uncomfortable. It's uncomfortable to be healthy and have an identity you're responsible for. It's much easier to pass it off on to someone else—even on to God.

To declare myself not to be true, to negate myself, to move about as a "walking contradiction"—this is a state of being that's common to my Christian thinking: I can't trust myself; I am full of bad fleshly things, therefore I have to constantly contradict myself if I want to experience what God wants in my life. I can remember as a child feeling guilty about anything that was tremendously fun. If it was that much fun, it had to be wrong. Consequently, I grew up learning to negate much of what was normal, healthy and gratifying in my human experience.

I am still working my way out of the sexual guilt of my adolescence in this regard. A normal adolescent stands on the brink of monumental sexual discoveries. The unexplained longings of awakening sexual hunger are a normal part of growth. Jesus must have had them, if He was human. I had them, and yet I learned to feel bad about them. I had them and negated them all at the same time. These kinds of negations hang on in later life and prevent us from being all that we are meant to be in Christ. Part of what we are meant to be in Christ, I believe, is a whole, sexual, human being.

I envy my son in this regard. He gets the benefits of our errors. He feels so good about his sexuality that he can't wait for puberty.

I can still remember my first wet dream—a warm, tingling flush followed by the greatest guilt I had ever known. (That might be related to the fact that I was awake at the time.) Having no one to talk to (no one ever asked), I continued to associate huge amounts of guilt with sexual experiences, imagined or real.

Had I been taught the truth about sexual realities, I might have come to more healthy conclusions about my own sexuality. Had I been encouraged to question God, I might have wondered why something that felt so good could be so wrong. I might have wrestled this out with Him until I concluded that my sexuality was the right feeling, and can be expressed at the right time. Instead, I learned to assume that the feeling itself was wrong. I learned to deny myself in the wrong way: to declare my bodily sensations to be wrong—and I became a walking contradiction.

If this kind of inbred guilt and fear was a design of my parents' generation to scare us away from sexual experiences, for me, at least, it worked. But only in a very limited way. I was never promiscuous and I've never had an affair—well, at least not a real one. I've had plenty of affairs of the mind, however. Yes, as a result of this philosophy, I can honestly thank my upbringing for making me a very safe, protected, twisted sort of a guy. Looking back, I would much rather have felt wonderful about my human sexuality and had to struggle with how I was going to use it or not use it. That's a much more healthy wrestling, and it's out front where I live, not concealed in the recesses of the mind where I'm trying to negate my basic nature and call bad what God calls good.

To deny myself, then, to take up my cross and follow Christ does *not* mean to impugn my humanity. It means to have control over it, and know when to tell it "no" and when to tell it "yes." Nor does it mean, as the third definition indicates, to disconnect myself in some way from myself—or as Webster puts it, *to disclaim connection with or responsibility for myself.* If I deny myself in this way, then I get to act as if I don't exist as a whole being: I can indulge in the flesh, but the flesh really doesn't count. I'm not really connected to it. I'm connected to the Spirit; the flesh is dead, it's not really me. Convenient though it is, this thinking is as old as the Gnostic heresy. Disconnected souls, wandering in a mist, longing for heaven, succumbing to earth: this is Dr. Jekyll and Mr. Hyde; this is spiritual schizophrenia. We go back and forth from flesh to spirit, from spirit to flesh. I can always say the devil or the flesh made me do it. If I've got myself all divided up into pieces, then I can arrange those pieces in any convenient way I choose.

Jesus did not go around cursing His flesh all the time. He sanctified it by the way He lived. He came not to negate life, but to live it. Jesus was connected to the Spirit of God *and* to His own humanity at the same time, and He found no conflict. Jesus Christ came *in the flesh.* If Jesus Christ was not fully human, then we cannot be fully saved and there is no ultimate hope for our humanity but to discard it completely and try something else. This is not what Jesus did. There is no "something else." This skin I live in is *it* for me, and it is what Jesus came to redeem.

I've always had the tendency to throw all of these things into one bad barrel: the flesh, the physical, the body and all of its bodily functions, the material . . . all of these things are thought to be sinful and anti-spiritual. To be spiritual, therefore, I must disconnect myself from them in some way.

When I did this, I never realized that the word *flesh* as it is used in Scripture is not always bad. It's true that flesh and blood cannot enter the kingdom of God, but my flesh is the earthly housing of my spirit, and when I die, and this body goes into the ground, it will be like a seed planted, so that a new, incorruptible body like Christ's body may spring forth in the resurrection. Just as a seed is connected to the body of the plant, so this flesh is connected to the eternal body I will soon wear (1 Corinthians 14:35–49). Right now, as you read this, Jesus Christ is sitting at the right hand of God in a resurrected body. Ten fingers and ten toes. He even bears scars from that earthly body, as Scripture tells us (John 20:24–29).

Your flesh—and *your* spirit. Have you learned to connect the two? Think about this. How you answer really matters. The scripture from which most of us derive our thinking on the matter is Romans, chapters 6, 7, and 8.

"But if Christ is in you," Paul instructs us, "your body is dead because of sin, yet your spirit is alive because of righteousness. And if the Spirit of him who raised Jesus from the dead is living in you, he who raised Christ from the dead will also *give life to your mortal bodies* through his Spirit, who lives in you" (Romans 8:10, 11) [italics added]. Because of the close proximity of the reference to the resurrection of Jesus in this passage, I've always assumed that giving "life to your mortal bodies" was about our eventual resurrection, as well. I'm not so sure anymore. Everything else in these verses is present tense. If this *giving life to my mortal body* can take place now, then it is my flesh Paul is talking about that can experience the resurrection power of the Spirit and be put to a good use. Indeed, I can operate in my flesh as a whole person honoring Christ when my mind is set on Him.

This, I believe, is the whole point of the first section of Romans 8—*that a mind set on fleshly things will be consumed by them, but a mind set on the Spirit of God will put the flesh (or the body) to its proper use.*

This is crucial to understanding what Paul is saying in these important chapters. Throughout Romans 6 and 7, Paul has made the point that my flesh is dead because of sin. Now in Romans 8, he is simply saying that my flesh—that is my mortal body—can come alive through the resurrected Spirit that lives in me, not some future day when my body goes into the ground, but right now, today, while I sip my morning coffee and reflect on these things and my heart beats blood and caffeine through my veins.

This same thought was strengthened already back in Romans 6:13, "Do not offer the parts of your body to sin, as instruments of wickedness, but rather offer yourselves to God, as those who have been brought from death to life; and offer the parts of your body to him as instruments of righteousness." If the parts of my body—that means even my sexual parts—can be turned into instruments of righteousness when presented to God, then I can be a whole, spiritual, human being and I do not have to disconnect myself from the physical in order to know this. If my flesh can be turned into an instrument of righteousness, then my body can be "played" by the Spirit, as it were. The flesh can be infused with life from the Spirit: and indeed this is the true meaning of sanctification—to put something to its intended use.

My flesh can praise God.

This remarkable fact is echoed many times throughout Scripture: Jesus Christ came *in the flesh*; Job declares that *"in my flesh* I will see God"; a man and wife become *one flesh* in marriage; and Paul declares that the life he lives *in the flesh* he lives by faith in the Son of God. These are arresting statements when you consider I have always assumed the term *in the flesh* had severely negative connotations. *In the flesh* was always synonymous with sinning.

Now I understand that when Paul talks about the negative aspects of the *flesh*, he is talking about the weaker element in human nature—the unregenerate state of man, the lower, fallen nature of man. He is not talking about skin. *Flesh* as a principle to live under is wrong; *flesh* as the skin I live in is right. It's the body I've been given that will be raised with Christ. It's the very image of God that I bear along with every other human being who's ever lived on this earth. It's the mortal body that can be given life through the Spirit. This flesh is *me*, and should I choose to have it so, it can become the very temple of the Holy Spirit of God.

This is me. This is all me. Grab it; pinch it. This flesh is me. This spirit is me. When I sin, it's me sinning. When I glorify God, it's me glorifying. I'm not watching this from someplace else. I'm not viewing—from a disconnected, irresponsible distance—the disembodied shell of myself; it's me here and I am choosing all the time what I am going to do with me. I am responsible. Cut my heart open and you won't find a throne-room with a miniature devil and angel playing musical chairs, you will find a heart beating for whom it wants to beat.

As Job has so beautifully and powerfully put it:

Oh, that my words were recorded,
that they were written on a scroll,
that they were inscribed with an iron tool on lead,
or engraved in rock forever!

(They were, Job, they were! You did it. We're reading them right now. You got your wish. Way to go, Job!)

I know that my Redeemer lives,
and that in the end he will stand upon the earth.
And after my skin has been destroyed,
yet in my flesh I will see God;
I myself will see him
with my own eyes—I, and not another.
How my heart yearns within me!

Job 19:23–27

This is all of Job wanting to know all of God. This sounds a lot like Jacob wrestling with God for his own real blessing. I hear burning passion that ignites even Job's flesh into a righteous fire.

In contrast to Job, I have come up with a modern Christian's corresponding yearning:

Poor wavering soul on the brink of sin;
Will he get out, will he give in?
Flesh and the spirit warring within . . .
What will he do, how will he win?

133

If only he could grab hold of his chin,
Unzip himself, and step out of his skin.
But alas, he finds, through thick and through thin,
That skin is the stuff he will always be in. . . .

The closer I get to truth, the simpler it becomes—deep in its ramifications, perhaps, but simple in its basic nature. Remember, only children get into the kingdom of God, so it can't be that tough. I notice that Paul finishes this very complex section of Romans with the most profound statement of grace recorded in Scripture—that nothing can separate us from the love of God. I now know that includes my past confusion over the complicated "subdivisions" of my soul.

When it comes down to it, there's really only God and me and what we do with each other. The more I mess with the simplicity of this basic two-part equation, the more excuses I end up making for myself not to burn with passion in my love for Him, not to wrestle with Him, not to lay hold of that for which He has laid hold of me. The more pieces I cut myself into, the more I dilute my love.

This tree outside my window, this big old gnarly thing, has had its own history. It has a huge gaping hole in its trunk, where it has fought, and is still fighting, some kind of fungus attack. It is susceptible to some insects and immune to others. Its leaves are a certain size and color unique to itself. No other maple tree had its roots down in this soil with this particular composition. Only this tree has experienced the weather pattern and growth pattern that has shaped its branches into what I view outside my window. If it was in a forest of maples, this tree would look much the same as the surrounding trees from a distance, but a closer examination would reveal its own identity.

My wife, as well, has her own identity: I've come a long way to answer her question. But it should be no surprise by now, considering how far it is from California to New England.

No, God would not ask Marti to deny who she is any more than He would ask this maple tree to be a spruce.

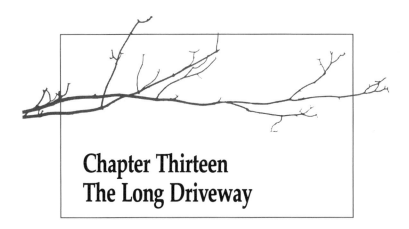

Chapter Thirteen
The Long Driveway

I'VE JUST READ an interview in *The Boston Globe Magazine* with Alain Briottet, Consul General of France, who was about to leave his post in Boston to become the French ambassador to Burma. He stated that the one thing he would miss the most about Boston was the snow, everything associated with the snow, and winter. He went on to say that the French poet, Baudelaire, felt the same way, that in winter, your mind is lucid and more able to deduce what to do. "It's a very good season to work," said Briottet. "Very crisp."

I agree, and should I ever leave this place for a warmer climate, I, as well, will miss the winter most of all. Winter forces everything inside. It invigorates. You think twice before you go outside. You cannot move freely from the inside to the outside. You have to stop and put on more clothes, then you have to stop and take them off when you get to where you are going. There's nothing casual about winter in New England. If you are going to be out in it, you had better be prepared.

You have to plan ahead, something I, as a Californian, have had to learn to do. When it's going to be below twenty degrees overnight, I have to plug in a heater that's connected to the engine block of the car so it will start up without running down the battery. I have learned how to get ingenious about things like this. For instance, I have a way of plugging in the cord so it can be controlled by the light switch in the garage. That's so all I have to do in the frigid early morning is step outside long enough to flick the switch on when I first get up, and the engine will be warmed by the time it's needed.

Or there's the heating wire that zigzags across the back edge of the roof so when ice builds up on the eaves as snow melts from the heat of the house, the water will have a place to run off instead of being forced back under the shingles by the ice blockage and leak into the house. I never knew water could run uphill until I came to New England.

And then we have to take extra precautions when we're going to be gone from the house for more than 24 hours, to guard against a freeze-up should something happen to the heating system. It already happened once and the ice burst a number of pipes that necessitated major repair work on the house. Now I hook up a clever little thermostat unit that attaches to a light that turns on automatically if the temperature in the house gets below a certain point. That way, at least the neighbors can catch the fact that something's wrong and get help before any major damage is done.

It's a good system because Debbie from next door keeps a close eye on everything. She knows all our goings and comings. We like knowing there are eyes on our place. We keep odd hours and are frequently gone. Debbie doesn't miss a trick.

Winter does have its setbacks, however. Thoughts driven inside sometimes go round and round, getting nowhere. We can often create problems and questions that aren't even there if we stay too long inside. I'm sure this is why God gave us seasons—winter to be inside, summer to be out—that we might understand the patterns and processes of life. Madeleine L'Engle has said that the reason we have time is so that everything doesn't happen at once. I also believe we have seasons so we can learn that life is not linear, it's cyclical, and each time around, hopefully, we circle deeper. The tracks of time cut further in—we go further in, in winter; and further out, in summer.

For Malcolm, though, it was the last time around. He died last night. He's been in winter a long time. I don't even remember when he last came out.

The ambulance came up the long driveway and left for the last time, carrying its frail package, little more than a crumpled leaf on the thin mattress. Alcena passed away a few months ago, and we all knew it would soon be Malcolm's turn.

No one was expecting Alcena's death, though. I took Debbie to the hospital in Boston to visit her, and watched the Giants and Cubs vie for the National League championship in the waiting room. No one on the hospital staff was overly concerned. She was strong and was in for a routine operation. Unknown to everyone, Alcena was only two days from death.

Yes, that was the big surprise. Alcena was the healthy one—still bright, active, wise and witty, still teaching nursery school and caring for her ailing husband. We all knew that with Alcena gone—Malcolm's only tangible reason for living—it would only be a matter of time. We had watched him fail considerably. We had watched him move deeper into the recesses of the house—from the porch to the living room to the bedroom.

Now they are both gone. This morning, only hours after his death, I watch the cars pass up and down the driveway outside my window just beyond the bare maple tree. These are not friends or mourners, they are parents dropping off their kids for what is now Debbie's nursery school.

Soon, children will be running and pushing and shoving their bundled little bodies in the snow and unraked November leaves, and the sound of their shouts will just barely reach my ears through the storm window, past the tree over here on the other side of the long, lonely driveway.

From a physical vantage point, Malcolm was a prisoner in his own home. His small world, to begin with, only got smaller. I could always count on Malcolm to be in one of two chairs, depending on the weather. If it was warm enough and not too humid, he would be out on the screened-in porch and I would wave to him from the rider mower each time I rounded the northeast corner of the backyard where a break in the lilac bushes affords a clear view of their house. If not, he would be sunk into the padded armchair in the living room that slung his hips lower than his knees, making them appear large and boney and in the same vicinity as his face. He read profusely, which may have been his path of escape—his wider world—but his physical reality was largely determined by two chairs and a bed.

Malcolm had become a specialist in restoration. In his early years, he built houses; in his later years, he dealt more in the past until he became known to us affectionately as The Restorer of Antiquity. For Malcolm, the past had become more promising than the future, which, according to his disease, was closing in on him at a steady pace.

What happened to Malcolm is what happens to anyone who attempts to live their born-again testimony over and over again and never have any fresh encounters with God, never question God, never seek to make real what they already believe. They always stay inside where it is safe and familiar, never venturing out. There are no soft chairs in the present or the future that lead anywhere but to a terminal ambulance ride.

Life closed in on Malcolm. He died of a disease that took his breath away. Malcolm, quite simply, ran out of air. I moved to New England to discover the value of the past only to find it suffocating—near death, now dead. I moved to New England to find what of my past faith could survive in the harsh, cold sunlight of the open world, only to find out that, quite plainly, none of it could. Faith is never a thing of the past. You can never use past faith for present challenges. Like the manna in the wilderness, faith is always present, always new. I can gain strength from the memories and memorial stones of God's faithfulness to me in the past, but my actual faith must always be a thing of the present. Present and active; always present and alive.

I found The Restorer of Antiquity, and then he died. Perhaps my search is coming to a close.

There is always a shortage of air for those who stay in one place. Life will not wait for us, nor will it offer us anything for existing. You and I are either in the flow or in bed, waiting for the air to run out.

God is more than a tube connecting fresh air to my nose as I try to survive a deadly world, waiting for the inevitable. He is the air outside, beyond the comfortable places. He will never supply air to the porch of rationalization where I explain away my inactivity, the soft chair of reprieve that postpones the wages of my sin, or the bed of regret that leaves me locked to the past and listless toward the future. He is the life beyond where I am living.

Outside my window, the stream of life moves on and God's doings in the world continue. With or without us.

Two more cars come and go, and the morning nursery school class exchanges with the afternoon one. Debbie chats with the parents from the porch and the familiar voice bounces merrily through the trees to my window. The children shout, laugh, and protest. Saturday, Malcolm's granddaughter will be twelve and the birthday party will go ahead as planned. Friday afternoon, my wife will take her to get her ears pierced, a promise made some time ago for her twelfth birthday.

We've heard there will be no funeral service.

The first week of April is almost history now and no sign of a bud forming. The view outside my window remains a mass of twisted brown, rocking in the wind—the only difference being an occasional bird streaking across the maze or pausing momentarily to hop through it. Not much hopping though; too much to do. The wind still blows a few brown November leaves, and but for the birds, and the absence of snow and ice, it's almost exactly the same view I've had for five months. Yet something has changed.

Yesterday, there was a hint of warmth in the wind. The sun was out for the first time in five days, and I heard there was a run on charcoal briquettes and lighter fluid at the country store. Today, the clouds and the wind's raw edge are back, but their grip is clearly loosening. Soon it will be time to hook up the long pipe across the backyard to the sump-pump in the cellar that will flush out the first thaw of spring. Soon bugs will buzz, eggs will hatch, warm rain will fall, and early morning dew will bead on green blades of grass. Soon life will be drawn outdoors. Soon . . . but not too soon.

It's impossible to mark the day one season passes. You cannot pick a date and put winter on one side of it and spring on the other. In New England, winter's passing covers a period of over two months—March, April and sometimes into May. On any one of these days, it could be 70 degrees and sunny or it could be 30 degrees and snowing, and usually it goes back and forth a few times, until it finally decides to stay warm. It's curious to me how you can feel spring's approach—almost feel the gargantuan movements of the earth tilting on its axis, putting the sun closer than it was yesterday. Winter will throw a few more spasms, but they are only death twitches. On any given year, it's impossible to know exactly when you crossed over a new line—you just suddenly realize that it's spring.

And now it's happening again. Here. I can sense it in the large movements of air, the outdoors has a fresh, living smell to it. It may look the same out my window, but it's not. Once in February there was a hurricane off-shore, and I went out in the backyard and smelled Florida. Somehow the tropical air was captured in the eye of the storm, carried a thousand miles, and flung out over Newbury, Massachusetts. I'm sure of it. Something like that is happening right now, because the air is not the same as it has been for the last five months, only this is not the result of an off-shore storm; this air belongs *here*, and will soon prevail. The movement cannot be stopped.

Normally, these first few warm winds, premonitions of spring, are enough to set one's spirit soaring on hope—but strangely, this time my spirit is reluctant to follow. It has been fooled by these winds before. I'm not ready for spring. Not yet. If spring comes too soon, I know I may be tempted again to put my hope in the wrong thing, like the crocus by our front door that trusts in the first hint of spring warmth, only to be frozen to death by an April snow.

The tree knows better. It's not going to let one or two warm days fool it into an early growth. If I want to be a tree, I can't put my faith in the first few warm sunny days that happen along. To do that is to trust the seasons of circumstance and not the presence of God in my life. Trees don't jump to conclusions about external circumstances; they don't need to—not with the huge root system they have sunk deep, spread wide over so many seasons of change.

I know for a fact that winter is not over with yet. And even if it were, it would be too soon at least for *me*. I haven't gotten all of what winter was here to teach me this time. An early spring tells lies: It tells me everything is better when it may not be. Tying my faith to the seasons—to warm airs or cold—is to live by circumstances and not by faith. It's letting physical things determine my reality and not spiritual things. That's why I came to New England in the first place. In California, it is as if it's spring all the time. In that environment, it's hard to tell if it's faith or just the weather.

Besides, I have premonitions right now other than spring.

I don't remember when I first realized that 24 Green Street was not going to be our permanent address. From the sense that we do not have an enduring city here on earth, nothing should ever feel like a "permanent" address—but I'm increasingly aware that our time here may soon be over.

In June, it will be seven years in New England. Jacob's life moved in blocks of seven, and I wonder if my identification with him runs deeper than I first thought. There are distinguishable rumblings of movement in my life right now, not unlike the ones that began this eastward adventure. This year's spring winds bear this premonition: that this will be the last time I will see the maple tree's bare branches; that the secrets and treasures are for another place, where what I have gleaned in this loneliness can sustain me. I know—in much the same way as I knew to come here—that it will soon be time to leave.

If these forebodings are true—and I have no reason to doubt them—then I must not give in to spring too soon. This may be my last chance to understand—to *get* what this winter is teaching me. I will stick with the tree whose roots are still locked many feet down into the frozen ground. . . .

These have been six lonely years.

For a good portion of this time, I interpreted the *loneliness* not as something I chose, but as something wrong. I fought with it long after I should have embraced what it was teaching me. I put so much energy into this move—into the self-motivation, into the physical nature of transporting possessions and preparing a home—that when all those activities were finally accomplished, I became deeply depressed. The vacuum that was left in my heart was like the sound of my feet on the wood floors of an empty house.

I wasn't prepared for the cavity that greeted me here. I

didn't hear my footsteps echo in an empty house and think, *Yes, this is what I came for—this is a good sound. The emptiness will mean that I can now distinguish God's voice from all the others.* No, what I was actually thinking in that moment was more like, *Holy Moses, what have I done? Did I leave God back in California? How come it feels so empty here?*

To tell the truth, I sort of half-expected to walk right into some great ministry here in New England. Perhaps I would become a modern-day Jonathan Edwards bringing this spiritually dark place back to its Puritan roots. Of course, this was just going to "happen." Like in the Jesus Movement, I would simply find myself in the right place at the right time. It would just come to me—the opportunity, that is—to have this kind of impact. When none of this happened, I began to feel even more concerned. For months, it seemed my footsteps went on echoing even after the furniture was in.

The first clear indication that we were having any kind of impact here was the first year we had a Christmas party and invited all the neighbors. Quite a few turned up. Perhaps they wanted to see what we had done to the Frost home, or perhaps they were curious what Californians would consider as Christmas, but they came in large numbers with all their kids. We had explicitly included children in this party. We found out later, this isn't usually done. Most Christmas parties here are dressy sophisticated affairs for adults only. Maybe people came just because we gave them a chance to include their children.

Marti, of course, was the coordinator of this event. Friends who were in town visiting us from California helped serve, making sure every plate and glass stayed full. One friend kept background music going on the piano most of the evening, ending with a glowing carol sing, with everyone crammed into the living room, dining room, and backed up against the front door—even up the stairs. Everywhere faces were flush with candlelight and joy.

The highlight of the evening was a surprise appearance by Santa Claus (Marti's dad, down from Maine), who delighted the younger children by peeking in all four frosty windows of the living room before bounding in the front door bearing gifts for every family and every child, complete with personalized name-tags. He also unrolled a large scroll, a calligraphy of a long poem, written by Marti and me, which included something personal about each family.

As the guests were all filing out at the end of the evening, one classic comment stuck with us. "Leave it to someone from California to show us what a real New England Christmas is like."

It wasn't exactly the impact I had in mind. So this was it . . . this was my great ministry? Not a spiritual revival—but a New England Christmas party? Was I missing it?

I thought I was missing the home Bible studies and the discipleship groups I was going to lead. I thought I was missing a great impact on our community for God. Mostly, I thought I was missing His will, and that my loneliness was the punishment. All along, I was only missing what He was trying to teach me in all of this.

I was missing the fact that our impact on the neighborhood was to come through simple things like this Christmas party, *and an awfully good one at that*. Our offerings were supposed to be small things. In fact, I had more to *receive* from being here than I had to *give*. God had to work something real into my life of faith before spring would ever come, and this winter of loneliness was not something to fight. All my connections would be on the inside.

Be still and know that I am God.

How do you learn to determine what to do next with your life, when people and circumstances have been determining it for you for so long? How do you start to trust your own voice when you've been conditioned to doubt it all your life? How do you ascertain God's voice, when it has always come through someone else, and now, suddenly, you find there is no one else around but you?

When a prophet of the Lord is among you,
I reveal myself to him in visions,

I speak to him in dreams.
But this is not true of my servant Moses;
he is faithful in all my house.
With him I speak face to face,
clearly and not in riddles.

Numbers 12:6–8

Moses got it straight. The rest of us have to get it un-
clearly and in riddles. You and I have to learn how to pick
His voice out of the clouds, how to unravel the riddle. But
how?

For me, it has begun by trying spiritual "muscles" I
knew I had—but have been afraid to try. I have begun—
and must continue—to trust myself more. And by that I
mean to trust my own ability to hear from God: to read His
Word and come to my own conclusions, and to believe that
inner sight. It is this primary contact with God—where the
fine root-fibres of my soul intermingle with the solid, sta-
bilizing nourishment of God's Spirit—that I have doubted
all along. So, ultimately, I have begun to trust God more,
and by that I mean to trust His ability to lead me in spite
of and including my mistakes.

"But you have an anointing from the Holy One, and all
of you know the truth" (1 John 2:20). That's *"all of you,"* not
just the smart ones, or just the leaders, or just the powerful
ones. All of you know *the truth*. This is a powerful anointing
that the Holy One has placed on all believers. Do we believe
this, or not?

In the early '70s, the Jesus music group Love Song had
a number of songs directed at unbelievers, gently urging
them not to listen to their intellect: "Listen to your heart
instead, and you will accept Him." I remember wondering
about that at the time, because my Christianity was full of
doctrines and creeds and truths and principles. I had always thought it was more important "what" you believed,
and the crucial thing was to "get it right" and make sure
everyone else did too. Thinking was always superior to any
intuitive feeling one might have. Intuition was suspect. My
initial reaction, therefore, was to be skeptical about Love

Song telling people to listen to their hearts instead of their heads. They were putting the whole process of revelation on shaky ground. Since when can we trust people's hearts?

I have now come to appreciate this sentiment, and to marvel at its wisdom. When I consider these lyrics were penned by "baby" Christians, less than a year old in Christian insight and teaching, I am forced to conclude that these words came not from theologians, experts in biblical truth, rational thinking, and Christian tradition but from the Holy Spirit.

This calling out to the heart was not just present in one song, it was a recurring theme early in Jesus music, confirming the call of the Spirit. One of my own early songs even reflected the same idea: "Have you seen Jesus my Lord?/ He's here in plain view./ Take a look, open your eyes/ He'll show it to you." Or consider the lyrics to another Love Song song: "Welcome back to the things that you once believed in./ Welcome back to what you knew was right from the start./ Sometimes you don't know what you're missing 'til you leave it for a while./ Welcome back to the love that is in your heart."

These lyrics were not devised by people seeking to sell music to a Christian market—there wasn't one yet—they were Spirit-breathed to a hungry, thirsty generation, and if the Spirit of God was reaching out to touch the heart of unbelievers, how much more can that same Spirit be trusted to speak and reveal truth in the heart of believers?

"As for you, the anointing you received from him remains in you, and you do not need anyone to teach you. But as his anointing teaches you about all things and as that anointing is real, not counterfeit—just as it has taught you, remain in him" (1 John 2:27).

In glaring contrast to this, so much teaching and preaching today betrays a lack of faith in the ability of believers to think for themselves or come up with their own conclusions based on this anointing of the Spirit. In the opinion of many popular Christian leaders today, believers apparently need someone else to do their thinking for them. In other words, Christians today are dumber than non-Christians were twenty years ago—at least it sure looks like that, from observing present ministries.

It seems to me that the anointing spoken of in 1 John gets sabotaged from two sides. But why? Is it that leaders don't like to tell people about their own ability to be taught of the Spirit because it makes those people less dependent on them? Is it that leaders are afraid of being stripped of some of their power and control? What if the Holy Spirit should reveal something contrary to what the leader says? Then the leader would have to be submissive to the people in this regard. . . .

At the same time, average Christian people sometimes don't like to hear about this anointing either, because it gives them more responsibility and that means they can't just sit back and let the professionals do it.

I have to conclude, for myself, that God is simply not going to accept the excuse: "But the pastor taught me such and such." To which I am now hearing Him reply, "But what did *I* teach you?"

According to John's teaching, we have all heard the inner voice of God. It's what called us out on this journey in the first place. We know what it sounds like: We know what it is to listen to it, and we know what it is to ignore it; to long for it, and to wish it would go away; to believe it, and to doubt it. But we don't simply trust it. No, not until we absolutely have to, until there are no other voices, until we are alone.

It was here in New England that I first started to trust my own ability to hear.

Through most of the '70s, I saw myself primarily as a teacher. A music reviewer once stated I was a teacher whose blackboard was music. I remember liking that and thinking it was an accurate description of what I was and what I wanted to be. I know now that it wasn't *all* I was to be.

I've finally realized, after much frustration, that there are two sides of my calling that have been, and will always be, in conflict. One side is the teacher in me that wants to make things clear; the other is the probing artist side that doesn't like everything cut-and-dried. The teacher loves to see that expression on a face when the light goes on; the artist hopes to challenge "reality" and see brows furrow in consternation. The teacher tries to simplify; the artist complicates. The teacher shines the light; the artist screams out from dark corners. The teacher lays out principles; the artist wants to know what those principles have to do with everybody's real life, and if it suspects the answer will be "nothing," then it will throw that unresolved bit of life back in the face of everyone's principle. The teacher loves truth; the artist loves beauty. The teacher talks about the way things should be; the artist reveals the way things are. The teacher coaxes reality into principles and lives as if it all fits; the artist holds reality up to the principle and knows it won't. The teacher deals more with the mind; the artist deals with the heart. The teacher runs on intellect; the artist runs on intuition.

The call to New England was heard by the artist in me. The artist wanted to paint beauty, shake up truth, and find reality. The artist wanted to stretch and explore, without having to defend itself to the teacher and those around him who understood only teaching. The artist hadn't had a chance yet to do anything for its own sake. The artist wanted to write a song that might or might not be a Christian song—might or might not be a ministry—might or might not fit into the teacher's scheme of things. It wanted to work somewhere out beyond definitions. Somewhere far enough away that it could not find its way back that easily. Somewhere, where trees go dead in winter, the artist heard the call and answered from the heart, from intuition, and was not understood very well by the teacher or many of his friends.

Six years in New England have given the artist room to stretch and somewhat balance out all the time when the teacher was in charge. It has been a time of building confidence in the intuitive gifts God has given me.

One thing I have noticed in this season is that the artist always seems to be ahead of what the teacher can articulate. I used to construct songs more as teaching tools. When the teacher writes a song, it's a controlled exercise. When the artist writes a song, it's more of a leap into new territory. Some of this can get downright scary. What comes as a result of this stretching are songs that I will usually be able to understand about two years *after* they are written. This kind of stuff makes the teacher very nervous, but he's beginning to trust the other in me.

It keeps happening—too often to be a coincidence. Songs I wasn't sure about two years ago, I'm singing with full confidence now. They seem to be directed at real deficiencies in the body of Christ or in my own life (and, consequently, in other people's lives), issues that desperately need to be addressed.

The clearest example of this is a song I wrote a couple years ago entitled "Too Many Preachers." The refrain has the following lines: "You've got to find it./ You've got to find it yourself./ None of these people [meaning, in context with the rest of the song, teachers and preachers] can give you any help." I wrote this song to encourage people to own their own faith. Teachers and preachers can *help* them in the process of finding the truth, but no one can help them believe. Believing has to be their own doing. What I was reaching for in this song, two years ago, is everything I am finding today. It's a strange feeling, to have a song suddenly hit me right between the eyes, and then realize I wrote it myself a few years ago, before I had full confidence in it.

This principle of capturing intuitively in music what I later discover in my thought processes is no new thing for me. The artist has been right before.

Twenty-four years ago, the artist picked up a guitar and sang from the heart, almost without thinking:

Look all around you and see what is real.
Hear what is true and be sure what you feel.

Touch someone near you in love, if you can.
Give all you have and be a part of God's plan.

Today, I realize this simple ditty (that, for years, I passed off as being an insignificant piece of writing—a somewhat juvenile camp song) was, in fact, a complete expression of my calling and my message. It has proven itself over all these years and I never saw it until now. You could almost say it is my own personal anthem. Everything I do and love is in here:

Look all around you and see what is real.
(The importance of embracing and addressing reality.)
Hear what is true and be sure what you feel.
(The importance of truth and the value of real feelings.)
Touch someone near you in love, if you can.
(The importance of relationships, love and vulnerability.)
Give all you have and be a part of God's plan.
(The importance of a passionate commitment to God.)

Twenty-four years ago, I didn't sit down to write a life-anthem. And yet I picked up my guitar and sang from my heart a tune that was to carry the essence of my message for the next twenty-four years—indeed, for the rest of my life, unless I hear differently. It has taken me this long to finally put faith in the voice that God has given *me*.

So now, when I pick up my guitar and knock out, "You've got to find it, you've got to find it yourself. . . ," I am starting to have faith in where that message is coming from. Is it time for many of us to start believing in our own gifts, our own "anointing," to make sure it's ours and not someone else's?

This is very scary business—this stepping out and trusting the intuitive, trusting the Spirit, trusting the heart, trusting the gift. Many would caution that spiritual intuition must be brought in line with the Word of God. I agree. But, ultimately, understanding the Word of God is up to me as well. Truth *in life* is not all cut and dried. No one group or teacher has a corner on it. Otherwise, someone could distill the truth into a three ring notebook for us and we wouldn't need the Bible any more. God's Word is something I can't simply take someone else's word for. I've got to know it myself.

So what happens to the teacher? Does the teacher die? No, the teacher still loves and searches the Scriptures to get to the truth. The teacher still clings whole-heartedly to answers. Will this inner conflict between teacher and artist ever be over? Probably not. The artist still questions those answers—in some cases, even tries to rip them away from the teacher's grasp. How then do I live with this? How do I reconcile these two warring sides of myself?

I don't. I have heard from God on this. Now that I have given large parts of my life to both I cannot deny either. I have heard from God on this and there will be no relief. This frustration I'm dealing with—this artist that wants to mess up what the teacher keeps trying to straighten up— it must go on, because out of the tension created by this conflict comes the message I am to give, in the way I am to give it.

And what is this message? I am to rip myself open and scream from every dark corner I can find in my life that God is Light. I am to reveal every lie in my heart and announce that He is true. I am to ask and *live out* every question I can find in my mind, and proclaim—with the question still etched on the lines of my face—that Jesus is the answer. I am to find out that the things I have always believed have come, not from some spiritual, abstract place where they have been tucked away for so long, but from some terribly human place—a place I have to know, to experience, to live through. If I do this, I will give someone else hope to believe from the place my message will find them.

> Remember how the Lord your God led you all the way
> in the desert these forty years, to humble you and to
> test you in order to know what was in your heart.
> Deuteronomy 8:2

Yes, I know it now: *I came to New England for the sheer human loneliness.* I say this confidently because I know I am in good company. Moses spent forty years alone in the desert before he was ready to set anyone free, John the Baptist was alone in the wilderness before he began calling the people to repentance, Paul spent at least fourteen years alone in Arabia before he began his ministry, not to mention Jesus, who was led away into the desert by the Spirit. They all went to a barren place—dry, lonely, deserted. They were directed there; it was part of the overall plan.

Why? I wonder. Why is this path traveled so often by holy men and women of God, even the Son of God? How about Jonah hiding under the withering shade of a vine, or Elijah hiding alone in a cave, being fed by ravens and lamenting his exile? What events in David's life led him to cry out the prophetic, "My God, my God, why have you forsaken me? Why are you so far from saving me, so far from the words of my groaning?" (Psalm 22:1). Was he simply providing something to do for seminary students who wanted to link up Psalm 22 with Jesus' words on the cross, or did he really feel this way—alone, deserted, forsaken?

Loneliness is not necessarily a bad thing. Loneliness can open the way to an intimate encounter with God. It trains the ear to listen for His voice, His song, His breath in the wind. It unclutters the horizon and sharpens the eye. It heightens the awareness of His presence as well as His absence. It makes everything all the more desperate. I've never prayed more in my life than since I moved to New England. But it hasn't been all prayers and answers. In fact, I'm not so aware of what I'm actually praying for. More like groping, touching, holding on to. My prayers are often wordless, emotive: The Great Longing, The Sure Knowing that lies at the bedrock of all the principles I learned as a young Bible student.

What has become important, in my aloneness here, is what comes at the end of each prayer, even the specific ones that ask for specific things. Not the answer, but The Presence, The Breath, The Enfolding. That makes any answer pale in comparison.

In these times, the closest thing to answers are tears.

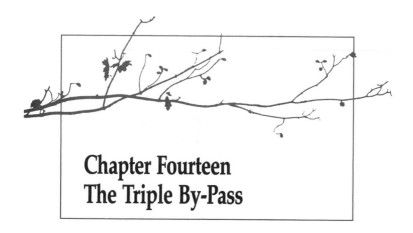

Chapter Fourteen
The Triple By-Pass

SPRING RAINS. THE CONSTANT DRIPPING. There's a heavy fog and mist today, which makes it feel as if the rain is not falling, but materializing in the air. Everything's soaked. Being in my backyard is like being inside the indoor-swimming-pool room of a cheap hotel with poor ventilation. The tree drips the heaviest drops, as if they wish to stay on its limbs a few seconds longer than anywhere else. Some fall on still-frozen ground, with old leaves sealed in patches of left-over ice, now pocked and dented with the heavy falling water-pellets.

Drops form everywhere. They grow by themselves on inanimate objects, mingle with their plump neighbors and finally fall off or run down the side of flat surfaces. It's as if everything is melting from the inside and pushing its way out. I don't think it's raining after all. It's *leaking*. Winter is seeping out from within.

"Got any water in your cellar yet?" asked Peter Himot, a friend in the neighborhood I have met through my wife's involvement with the YWCA. Our wives are always volunteering us for community projects, and in the course of moving tables and chairs around we've developed a relationship of sorts. I say this because a "relationship" with Peter is a little like a one-way street with all the cars coming at you.

"It's going to be a wet spring. Better get your sump-pump hooked up." Peter is always checking up on me. He's convinced that we Californians are not going to be able to survive the demanding elements in New England. And he *is* helpful, it's just that sometimes I wish he would be a little *less* helpful.

"Your roof is looking pretty shabby over there under the right dormer": He'll say this kind of thing—frequently. He'll drive by slowly, see me out in the front yard, stop his van, get out, come over and tell me something that's wrong about what I'm doing, or something *else* I should be doing when I'm done with the thing I'm busy with at the moment. "One more winter of ice-block and you're going to have one huge leak up there."

Peter is an expert at what's wrong. Whether you want to know or not, he'll tell you what's wrong with everything from the country to your kitchen sink. To his credit, for everything he points out that's wrong, he also has a solution for it, and usually a pretty good one at that. Peter's thing, actually, is to solve problems. He knows how to fix most things.

I, on the other hand, have my own private way of doing things, and I resist any suggestion that there might be a better way. I prefer to call Peter when I'm really in trouble—when I've used up all my options—than to have him pull up in front and give me a piece of unsolicited advice that I would just as soon not know about. If my solution isn't going to work, I'd like to find that out myself.

When I call him up on the phone, it's always the same, "Himot here." That's the way he answers the phone. It's hard to believe that there would come a day when I would call that number and not find Himot there. I might find his wife or maybe his sons there if they were in town, but I would never again find Himot here, or Himot there, or Himot anywhere, for that matter.

You either have one of two reactions to Peter and to other people who are like him. You either tolerate them and listen to all they have to say for the truth that it holds, or you wish they would go away. Most people wish Peter would go away—especially at parties. I suppose it might have made Peter a little more tolerable for all of us if we had known that our wishes would come true so soon.

Watching Peter at a party is like watching the negative pole of a magnet move about a mass of negatively charged pieces. Peter's idea of dressing up for a party is to grab a shirt (any shirt) and a tie (any tie), cover it with a coat (any coat), thrown over corduroy pants and an old pair of Earth Shoes (remember those?). He has a freckled face, and wiry reddish gray-blonde hair that springs out of the sides of his head where he can still grow it. His mind is constantly working over whatever you are talking to him about so that it spills over into a nonverbal twitch or a sort of half-whisper of the very words you are saying while you say them. Sometimes it even seems he mouths your words ahead of you as if he reads your mind and knows what you're going to say before you say it. Sometimes you wonder why you bother to have a conversation with him at all, since he manages the whole thing. To talk to Peter is to have Peter IN YOUR FACE! Once you start talking to him, it's hard to get out of the conversation. You feel cornered.

Marti handles him very well, however, perhaps better than anybody, because she knows how to do this, too. They've been known to go at it for some time, throwing it back and forth in each other's face. Because of this, Peter and Marti have a kind of "thing" together that I don't understand—a mutual IN YOUR FACE! kind of thing.

I've finally figured out that all this IN YOUR FACE! stuff—and this confronting that Peter does—is because he really does care. He presents these solutions because he wants to solve your problem. When I phone him with a question and hear his characteristic greeting—"Himot here"—he means just that. Himot is really "here"—here for you—a lot more "here" than a lot of other people I know, Christians included. When he's *here*, he's *here for you*, if you are a friend and need him. I can't always say that much for myself.

"I noticed you've got some bricks coming loose in your front steps there. A twenty-five-pound bag of cement should take care of that. Cost you under five bucks."

Peter has turned into a hero of sorts, the town advocate for the young-and-the-restless of Newbury. The odd hair-cuts, chains and black jackets can often be seen hanging around his house. He once went on a campaign to get the city to provide a skateboard park, instead of outlawing the activity altogether, which is what they wanted to do. When this failed, Peter let his kids build a skateboard ramp on their front yard—an eyesore in the community and Peter's personal snub at the town.

I'm sure much of this has to do with the fact that Peter still has a lot of the young-and-the-restless in him. He challenges life head-on and is sometimes very stupid about this. Like when he had a triple by-pass and went right back to stuffing cholesterol into his system. Peter is not going to die bored, that's for sure. And when he does die, he's the kind of person who's going to have a few words with God, regardless of where he ends up.

There would not have been a place for Peter in the Christianity of my childhood, except to be an object for witnessing to or an example of the depravity of man. He would have been looked at as an obnoxious sinner, one who left no doubt as to his degenerative nature. He would have been type-cast and judged and written off as a lost cause—a crude, opinionated non-God-fearing atheist. Certainly he would be one person a fine Christian like me would not want to call a friend. Yet here in New England, where friends do not necessarily grow on trees, he and his wife have turned out to be very loyal to us.

No one would ever come right out and admit this, but most Christians act as if non-Christians are to be either witnessed to or ignored, but by all means, don't have them over for dinner.

Actually, the Himot's have had *us* over a number of times for dinner, but the most memorable have undoubtedly been the times we were invited to join in a Passover meal. Peter's family is Jewish, and though his own personal orthodoxy is in question, the traditions still stand. What a privilege it has been for us to share in *this* inner circle, where the promises to Abraham, Isaac and Jacob live on around a twentieth-century dinner table and the story of Moses and the children of Israel is still told again and again and again, and the angel passes over one more time.

It doesn't appear that Peter cares a whole lot about the absence of blood on the doorpost, but that does not make him and his family any less blessed. On Passover, we share in the stories and the meal, and my son, Christopher, prays the youngest son's prayer because he is the youngest son in the room. Then I am aware that Peter is a blessed man in ways I cannot know. The blood of Abraham flows in him. The blessings and curses of his fathers are lived out in his life. And somewhere in his soul, Jacob and Esau still wrestle. One has the other by the heel, only this time I do not know which one will win.

There is a grand human dignity to Peter: a tragedy and a glory to his independence.

The glory is that God created us not as robots and spiritual weaklings, but as men and women in His image. That includes the freedom to exercise our own will—to come after Him or ignore Him. It is in coming after Him, in our own way, that we discover both a relationship with Him and our own value. We wrestle something of our own dignity out of the experience of meeting God—and lo and behold, God lets us have it! He gives us the blessing, like He gave it to Jacob. He lets us win, as it were. God allows us self-respect and honor. We may walk away from an encounter like this with a limp (never to forget with Whom we have struggled), but we walk away as well with dignity and with a Friend. For you have met God and yet your life is spared.

The tragedy is that, even in walking away from Him in

disbelief, we are no less dignified. When He was here on earth, Jesus treated all human beings with the same value and dignity, the same value and dignity He gave us when He made us. God treats us with more respect than we generally give to each other. God allows us to wrestle with Him—to win, or to lose—and to walk away claiming something as our own. God allows us to walk away and have nothing to do with Him, and though the results are devastating, the latter may be an even greater statement of His love than the former.

Psalm 8 contains the following:

> When I consider your heavens,
> the work of your fingers,
> the moon and the stars
> which you have set in place,
> what is man that you are mindful of him
> the son of man that you care for him?
> You have made him a little lower
> than the heavenly beings
> and crowned him with glory and honor.
> You made him ruler over the works of your hands;
> you put everything under his feet:
> all flocks and herds,
> and the beasts of the field,
> the birds of the air,
> and the fish of the sea,
> all that swims in the paths of the seas.
>
> Psalm 8:3–8

Who is this that is crowned with glory and honor? Who is this with everything under his feet? This is man, the one who is "a little lower than the angels." This is not the Son of Man, this is the lower case son of man—every man and woman "crowned with glory and honor."

This is Chuck walking slowly down my driveway headed to a Tuesday night ballgame. This is Phillip having someone screen all the FAX messages in his office. This is Peter racing downhill on an advanced ski slope defying bypasses and warnings and cholesteral counts. This is Marti negotiating with a CEO on her car phone. This is my friend on his way to an A.A. meeting. This is Peter, careening off the advanced run—off into the trees somewhere, his heart making its own new defiant trail in his chest. This is Debbie welcoming her nursery school children for one more day of school with the same cheery lilt in her voice as if it were the first day. This is John sitting across from Debbie's porch, watching through empty branches from my place by the window. This is Peter, son of the blessing, doing last second business with angels as he is pulled out of an icy river, and this is his son, crying over the limp, cold body. This is man, crowned with glory and honor, and this is heaven, aching in the tragedy and the glory of it all.

"You know what those are?" I remember Peter asking me one spring after the first truly warm days. "They're carpenter ants. You know why they call them carpenter ants? Guess. You'd better get a bug guy in here before they chew up your whole foundation. That can of Raid is not going to get you anywhere."

"John, you better fix your garage doors before they fall on somebody. It's the doorposts. They're not fastened in well enough to hold up the heavy doors. Speaking of falling, that apple tree by the driveway is going to go during the next storm. You know that don't you?"

And wouldn't you know, it did.

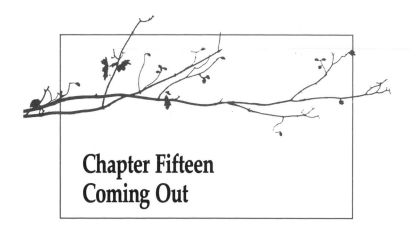

Chapter Fifteen
Coming Out

IN TRUTH, THE WHOLE APPLE TREE didn't go, just half of it. The storm literally tore the tree in half and dropped one side of it clean across the driveway. It was a mortal wound. The exposed cavity, once inside the trunk, was now in full view. You could see where the side that split off had given way from a good deal of rotting from the inside—and yet the back side, the half-round of the remaining trunk, seemed to still hold some strength.

As I chain-sawed the fallen sweet smelling apple wood that was blocking the driveway, I half-expected to see Peter's familiar blue van pull up—half-thought I heard his shrill voice in my ear, warning me that I had better cut down the rest of the tree before it falls on somebody. But it was only the sound of the noisy chain saw whirring.

Peter was good for me. His crusty character always forced me to confront the uncomfortable. As a rule, I've never been good at confrontation.

God, I miss him.

My family had an unwritten rule: Never say anything that might make anyone feel uncomfortable. I have since found this is typical of most families of my era. Try as I may, I just can't picture Ozzie putting his fist through a door as Harriet comes apart at the seams. The closest Ozzie ever got to a real feeling was to wave his arms around and whine in the upper register with a constipated look on his face, while Harriet kept on smiling and dicing vegetables in the kitchen. Not a pretty sight, but my generation grew up with it on TV and at home. Add to this the expectations of a "Christian" family, and you can have real feelings buried to an almost irretrievable level.

Christians are *not supposed to* have conflicts; they are *supposed to* always be at peace with each other. These *supposed-to's* and *not-supposed-to's* are the greatest enemies of real faith that I know of. The way we are *supposed to* be and *not supposed to* be will always keep us from seeing and facing the way we *really are*.

Marti has been a real challenge for me in this regard, for she has absolutely no respect for these cherished Christian personality suppositions. She never learned how to avoid conflict so as to maintain an *appearance* of peace. She never learned how to buffer her emotions, keep all of her uncomfortable feelings inside, and come out with a nice, harmless, *supposed-to* response. Sometimes I find myself longing for just a few good *supposed-to's* just for a break. ("Come on—fake it a little for me, honey—just for old time's sake.")

Consequently, if Marti is mad, what I usually get is anger; if she's depressed, I get depression; if she's frustrated, I get tears, screams and I've even been hit by flying objects and a few flying fists; if she's excited, I get excitement. I say *I* get these things, because I am usually the closest thing to her when they occur and often I am the cause. My constipated, whining Ozzie imitation only makes her want to pound harder to get something real out of me. (How could you *ever* take a guy named Ozzie seriously?)

The point here is not merely the expression of real feelings. Marti is not some emotional dingbat flailing away until she gets some feeling out of me; she is not advocating an emotional encounter session where you pound on pillows and feel better for it because you "got in touch with" your true feelings. She is trying to get me to connect to something real inside myself. She's trying to get me out of the abstract and into the concrete. She is trying to get me to break through my *supposed-to's* and *not-supposed-to's* and face the problem. Dealing constantly with what I am *supposed-to* and *not-supposed-to* do keeps me from ever having to *do* anything.

Today, what we were *actually doing* was having a real live conflict. *Not-supposed-to's* were flying around the room and clogging my brain, making it harder for me to connect with what was happening—because according to my presuppositions, this whole tense scene was *not-supposed-to* be happening.

The details of our conflict are irrelevant now. Most of our clashes spring from the same elements. Marti is a born leader. She inspires, motivates and keeps everyone oriented toward the big picture. She has no patience for anything more detailed than an outline. Got to keep everything moving and everyone engaged. She sets things up, and then moves on to something else and gets impatient when people can't keep up with her. This works great in an office, but at home it's a different story.

At home, Marti knows that she can push and pull forever, but if I'm not engaged it's not going to happen. We always seem to walk into these conflicts from entirely different perspectives. Marti has been out painting bold brilliant murals on the walls of the world, moving around large quantities of people, money and ideas; I have been picking through words on the small screen of my computer, moving around pieces of sentences with a tiny pointed cursor. I have to back out of the infinitesimal, and she has to back down from the grandiose in order for us to meet anywhere.

Her major problem with me, I will admit, is getting me

to engage in anything outside my own comfort zone, which is often about the size of a computer screen.

She had been acting for some time now on the presumption that God was leading her, but as of yet, there had been no external confirmation of that fact. Nothing was coming out concrete. How long does she have to wait? She was not in this particular race for the long distance. There are other long distance races she is able to endure, but she never signed up for *this* one. If He could just give her a sign, even "1/4 OF A MILE TO GO," she could hold on, but this time she was running out of gas.

"Okay—so I'm learning patience," she said. "I'm learning to accept controls on my own conduct, but how long does this go on before I see some light? I am not a cute manipulating person. I can't do this any other way unless God does something on my behalf. I've had enough. I can't take it anymore.

"And where have *you* been?" she challenged. "You're either on the road, or you're up there staring into your little computer screen. Why do I always have to create a scene like this to get your attention? I'm not blaming you, I just want you to *do* something. Is this the rest of my life? Does it end like this?"

Now in the past, when one of these sessions has begun, I have usually found myself mentally starting up a long, involved road of rationalizations. Something like:

1. This is *not supposed to* be happening. I can't deal with this.
2. Who does she think I am—Houdini?
3. Why is it always *my* fault?
4. Of course, *she* hasn't done anything to get us into this situation.
5. What time is it anyway? Don't we have to leave now?
6. Didn't I have devotions today, God? Why is this happening to me?
7. There goes the perfect marriage.

8. Why can't she be more spiritual?
9. That's probably my fault. I'm not being a good husband.
10. I knew it. We should never have left California.

Of course, as I walk through this process, I'm no longer listening. I'm pulling myself further and further away from Marti, until her voice is nothing but a distant murmur. At this point, I am fully into myself and of no immediate use to Marti or the conversation. The longer this goes on, the smaller I become, until, in my own eyes, I am a pea of a person. She does not do this to me; I do it to myself. It's a fleshly way of protection from having to get out of myself and into the problem. It's the process I have developed for avoiding conflict. I distance myself from it; I shrink as a flesh-and-blood man. It's too uncomfortable for me to go through this, so I leave the room without leaving the room.

The murmur usually continues until we wear each other out—she with her frustrations, me with my rationalizations. I know this pattern well.

This time was different.

This time as I listened to Marti, I began to feel her frustration. I started to see it from her point of view. Things I formerly would have taken personally I let go by. This time I engaged; locked on. And the more I heard, the more I took on her hurt and frustration, the more I forgot about my *self*. Then *I* became frustrated, because I wanted to do something, but there was nothing I could do.

This time I stayed in there and listened to her. And suddenly I was reminded of all the reasons why I love her so much. Suddenly, the differences that before would have driven me away brought me closer. I wanted to embrace her and all of our problems and do something about it. Yet the closer I got, the more uncomfortable it became, until my own frustration found an expression that shocked us both. I'm not even sure where this statement came from— it was so out of character for me—but I do think Jacob had something to do with it. I suddenly shouted out loud:

"HEY GOD, IT'S NOT FAIR FOR YOU TO JERK MY WIFE AROUND LIKE THIS!"

We both looked at each other for a moment in disbelief and then we started laughing. I could hardly believe myself. I had never talked to God like this before. You weren't *supposed-to* do this. You were *supposed-to* be nice around God. Tiptoe. Speak quietly and reverently. None of this "HEY GOD, IT'S NOT FAIR. . . !" I waited for the lightning, but it never came.

"Do you realize what you just did?" Marti said, already brightening somewhat. "You stood up for me in front of your biggest audience."

"I guess I did," I said, still unsure of what actually happened.

"How do you feel?" she asked, wiping around her eyes.

"I feel great," I said. And then we hugged each other and we cried and laughed some more, kind of at the same time. And though nothing about the situation was solved, something about us was like it had never been before.

She was right. I did stand up for her in front of my biggest audience. For once, I short-circuited a *not-supposed-to*. I acted before a *not-supposed-to* had a chance to take effect. It makes me think of how many times I have short-circuited my real self in the process of trying to give God what I *thought* He wanted—when all along what He wanted was my real self. All those times I tried to do it right, but He wanted a relationship with the real me, not a performance. It's all Marti seems to want, too: a relationship with the real me, not the *supposed-to* me.

I wonder how many times I have been in God's presence feeling one way, but saying something else, some stupid words that meant nothing to me because I was afraid to tell Him how I really felt? Or maybe I didn't even know how I really felt, I just gave Him a pat expression. I mouthed words I'd heard somewhere before, failing to connect with myself, and failing to connect with Him. I wonder what He really wants to hear.

I believe He wanted me to share in my wife's emotions

that day and not distance myself from her as I'd previously done. Her feelings were appropriate to our life right then. I'd known for a number of days that this was building. There was no way she wasn't going to crack at some point over what we were going through. These were not just her feelings; she was saying it for us. I knew, too, that if I took on her emotion I would feel just as frustrated and I would have nowhere to turn. Something tells me that's exactly where God wants me to be.

It's an uncomfortable place to be—having no defenses, but putting yourself out there anyway. It must be a little bit like the first buds of spring pushing their way out of brown brittle twigs, trusting the huge movements of the earth, letting the sap begin to flow again, embracing all of life in its shapes and forms, ups and downs, pains and joys.

I'm ready to take all of this. I'm ready to embrace what I don't know or can't control—to call *mine* what is mine, even in the face of my inadequacy. I'm getting ready to come out again.

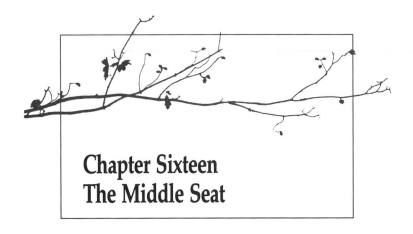

Chapter Sixteen
The Middle Seat

*But Esau ran to meet Jacob and embraced him; he threw his
arms around his neck and kissed him. And they wept.*
Genesis 33:4

I WOKE UP THIS MORNING to a brisk spring day. Rain
had been falling on and off for three days, but somewhere
in the night the clouds dissipated, leaving behind a sparkling washed wetness. During my early morning ride to
the airport, the bare trees were shaking themselves off onto
my windshield like dogs after a bath. Some of them were
starting to sprout feather-light growth that reminded me
of how I used to make trees for my electric train layout
when I was a kid by shellacking small tree-shaped twigs
and then shaking them in a paper bag full of little bits of
green yarn.

I got a good look at the maple before I left, and though
it would be sprouting by the time I returned from this trip,
this morning it was only freshly shellacked by the rain—
not tacky enough yet to be shaken with green. As far as I
can tell, maples are among the last trees to trust that spring
has truly come.

A long day in planes and airports awaited me. Flight

#67 was going to take me to San Francisco in three tries. First to Washington D.C. , then to Kansas City, then finally to the City by the Bay. Same plane all the way. Same seat: 21E, which, for those of you familiar with flying, is a middle seat. The first leg to Washington was full, but the other two flights had some empty seats, so I got up and stretched a little at each airport and took a different seat when I reboarded, my preference: an aisle seat.

The last leg from Kansas City to San Francisco was the sparsest, so I started down the aisle, looking for the perfect seat. I had my eyes on a whole row, so I could lower all three tray tables and turn the place into my temporary office, with folders, lap-top computer, reference books and airline meal all handy in front of me. *Sure John, take it. An aisle seat with an empty middle isn't enough, you've got to have the whole row.* Glancing around the plane, however, I found plenty of other vacant rows and told that voice to get lost.

Feeling fortunate, I leaned my head back and started thinking about my earlier days in the '70s at Peninsula Bible Church—the inner room, the dinner with "Umgawa" on top of the space needle, the last conversation with my mentor on the redwood deck—they all came back to me vividly as I anticipated returning to the Bay Area. This was an uncustomary trip—not my usual appearance at a concert, or a retreat, or a Christian college. I was going to be singing a few songs as part of a special evening to honor over forty years of ministry by one very faithful and gifted man. I was going to help countless people, myself included, to thank a man for being a very important example in their lives.

What do you say when your leader retires? Do you joke about "Umgawa" riding his last wave? How do you make this significant? How do you thank a person for forty years of ministry? Shall I sing all the old songs—memories of the Jesus Movement of the '70s? This retirement pow-wow was going to be ripe with nostalgia. I knew I would not be the only one going back to dance one last dance with my past.

Suddenly I remembered the first time I'd ever heard

Love Song sing the soothing, haunting harmonies of "Welcome Back," not on stage with all their gear, but in the pastor's study with just a guitar, singing for a few members of the staff and elders. We had wanted to hear them sing to check them out before an evening service, something done with all guest singers. After all, we'd never heard of these guys before. So Chuck Girard started strumming his gut-stringed guitar and, there in the inner room, they all closed their eyes, lifted their long-haired faces and sang, "Welcome back to the things that you once believed in . . ." When they were done, there wasn't a dry eye in the room. After a long silence, I remembered someone saying, facetiously, "Yeah . . . that will do."

Then there were the times Hal Lindsey happened to be in town, or once when Eldridge Cleaver came by to give his testimony shortly after his conversion, and we in the inner circle had to keep these appearances a secret because the service was already packed—a success due not to the presence of famous people, but to the famous presence of so many ordinary people.

I closed my eyes on my way to San Francisco, alone in row 21 on flight #67 from Kansas City, and I was again on the modest stage of an unpretentious church, which was packed, literally up to my feet, with eager young faces. I was singing a brand new song, with the lyrics freshly taped to the mike stand. I looked out over those faces in my daydream and remembered a real family. That was when I first truly understood what Jesus had meant when He said, "Here are my mother and brothers. For whoever does the will of my Father in heaven is my brother and sister and mother." It was on this stage that I first related my discovery that women could be sisters and friends without being potential mates, a teaching that is still setting others free to enjoy deeper relationships with one another. I wondered what I would say and sing from that stage this time, so many years later.

I wondered how many of my old friends would be there this weekend and what it would be like to see them again.

Had they found it necessary to rediscover their faith as well, or is this only my journey? Are they all back there in the same place I left them or have they moved on? Do you have to go to New England to get this? Does it always take seven years?

By now I was feeling a mix of nostalgia and nervousness. How would I stand in the place where I had stood so many other times and not be intimidated by my own past? How would I face the Esaus of my own life, these people I'd left behind by the circuitous course of my own choosing? And how would they all react to seeing me?

I opened my eyes to see the back of the middle seat in front of me and noticed a newspaper folded up in the seat pocket. Knowing we'd made so many stops, I wondered where it might be from. I'd seen a lot of *Washington Posts* after we left Washington National Airport. Or it might be a Kansas City paper that would give me a mid-western perspective on the world. Of course it wouldn't be the San Francisco Chronicle; not yet. I started thinking how I would soon be able to see the Chronicle again. I love newspapers and the particular identity they bring to the various places I have lived. One of my prized possessions is a personal letter from Herb Caen, well-known columnist for the Chronicle, complimenting me on my last book. I keep it framed above my desk next to the baptismal picture, my sort of worldly credential.

I reached into the seat pocket in front of me and pulled out the newspaper. The familiar banner of the *Boston Globe* greeted me. *How did this get on the plane?* I thought. Then I remembered: This flight began in Boston. I brought a *Globe* on board; I always do on morning flights.

Wait just a minute. I quickly got up out of my seat, fished the airline ticket out of my coat pocket in the overhead bin, and returned to the middle seat I had commandeered into an office—the seat I'd settled on after moving twice around this plane. I checked my boarding pass and found my assigned seat was 21E. The row sign above me read . . . 21E! I suddenly felt like Michael Keaton trying to tell Kim Bassinger that he was Batman. I moved my lips, but nothing came out: "This is . . . *my* . . . seat . . ." I mouthed, looking around at no one, sharing an astonished laugh with only God and myself.

Imagine, I had felt guilty about taking what was rightfully mine!

As I sat there chuckling inside, I knew this little episode was a scripted finale on the last seven years of my life: stealing my way back to what belonged to me all along. God had played a joke on me, and the smile on my face lasted all the way to San Francisco.

In that joke was all the information I would need to face the Esaus of my memories. How do you stand up in a place where you've stood so many times before, but for other reasons? How do you keep from losing all you have gained from being on your own? How does the man return home without becoming the boy his parents thought they put on a train months, or maybe years, earlier? How do you keep from falling under other people's shadows? There's only one way: You stand in your own sun. From its light, you draw strength for roots that are deep and seasonless. You overthrow your intimidation and your fear of so many hairy Esaus and return to your former home with a blessing that you have wrestled for yourself by going hand to hand with God. You end up loving every person you see and every memory that seeing them holds for you, because you are no longer fighting them or your memories to find out who you are and what you are to do. You know that now, and it has nothing to do with them. It has everything to do with you and God.

Though I would later walk off Flight #67 into one of the most exciting weekends of my life, nothing else was as important. I went on to be warmly and lovingly received by everyone at the church. I knew just what to sing and what to say, as I do now on any other stage. I wept as I looked on the faces of my friends and realized I loved them still. I discovered how everyone else had grown in their own way. One teacher I had always thought so stoic and mechanical (the antithesis of an artist), was now quoting poetry . . . his own. The ethnocentricity of my concentration on the '70s was put into perspective by stories of the effects of a faithful man's ministry during the '50s, the '60s, and the '80s as well. I even sat in my mentor's car and recalled our conversation on the deck of my California home seven years earlier—and was honest about my failures, and bold enough to point out a few of his. Yes, I returned to the inner room and found it cluttered with an extra desk and a couple of computers, and while we prayed there, with barely enough room to stand, I realized that there wasn't anything more sacred about this room than any other room I've prayed in before any other meeting. I found the sacred thing, not in my memories, not in a room, but in me and in the *present-tense faith* of those who stood praying around me.

It didn't really matter what happened after I discovered I was in my own seat. I kept looking at that boarding pass, just to see it. Sure enough: 21E. I'd been assigned this seat from the airline, and I'd sat there dutifully, squished between two other quiet commuters from Boston to Washington. I travel almost every weekend, so I understand this industry; I try to cooperate as much as possible. I'm probably one of the few who actually watch the safety demonstration. I even watch it when it's on video. I am a model passenger.

For years, I was a model Christian. I was familiar with all the demonstrations; I could give the speech myself. I sat in my assigned seat and took it willingly. Seven years ago, I left my seat—not the plane, just the seat—and I took other seats, of my own choosing. All the way to Kansas City, I explored the plane from different vantage points, and when I had seen enough, on the last leg of the trip, I finally chose the seat I wanted; and as we landed in San

Francisco, what was once my home, I realized that in leaving, I had come home to what was mine all along. It was my seat. It has been my seat for the whole flight. This time, though, it was different, because I chose it. That made all the difference in the world.

Chapter Seventeen
Full Leaf

Arise, my darling,
my beautiful one, and come with me.
See! The winter is past;
the rains are over and gone.
Flowers appear on the earth . . .

Song of Songs 2:10–12

Daughters of Jerusalem, I charge you:
Do not arouse or awaken love
until it so desires.

Song of Songs 8:4

THE WARMER AIR is forcing me to unstick the composition storm window across from my desk. I realize I've been viewing the scene out my window through dirty glass for the last few weeks. The build-up must have been so gradual that I never noticed it happening. I had nothing else to compare it with until today, as I wash off a winter's worth of muck. There's nothing quite like the first spring day when you can open windows.

Sliding the outer panel open is like releasing the dead. I imagine the air trapped there all winter between two panes of glass—never changing, never moving. Storm windows provide an extra layer of protection, but they also incarcerate a few little critters who never realized their home was going to become a tomb. That which insulates is also that which houses the dead and leaves its residue to cloud the view.

I wrestle the frozen panel loose, and the dead air is swept away instantly. Skeletons of insects blow out of the corners and float down along with seedlings from the maple tree that have collected on the window sill. These catch the back-draft and spin in the air like tiny helicopters.

Then I wash off the graveclothes. On the outside are water stains from spring rains and the successful dive bombings of what must have been a squadron of birds. Trapped in the middle are vacated spider webs, tiny balls of insect larvae, fly excrement and vacant cocoons. On the inside, grime from the woodstove, fingerprints of children, residue from soft sticky toys made to cling to any surface when thrown, round circles left from licked darts that hit their marks—and everywhere, the dust of life. All these dissolve in the Windex of spring, vanish in the sparkling sunlight that now stands framed in the window pane.

Before I wipe it all off, however, I can't resist the temptation to leave the dirtiest part of the window, the outside, just long enough to step back into the room and see what it looks like with "JOHN IS GREAT" scrawled on it.

It looks terrific.

There's going to be a wedding.

It's not just a window I'm cleaning, it's a lens, and since it's a lens to the outside, I feel like I'm cleaning the whole world. That's all that's necessary, you know. We're not going to clean up the world, but we can clean up the lens through which we look at the world and others who live in it. "He who seeks good finds goodwill, but evil comes to him who searches for it" (Proverbs 11:27).

A lot of people are looking for evil these days. Is it any wonder that they are coming up with it? I think we could stand a bit more window cleaning and a lot less demon hunting. It's amazing what a little Windex will do. We're always trying to fix up somebody else's place, while neglecting our own dirty windows. Pretty soon, someone's going to notice how dirty our windows are and suggest to us that this might be why the world looks so bad.

"He who seeks good finds goodwill." Jesus found it in the most surprising places: in a young boy who desired to share his lunch, in a Roman soldier's faith, in an outcast Samaritan woman, in the sinners and tax collectors at Levi's house—in the madmen and lepers and lame and numb and dumb, he found goodwill. "Peace on earth to men of goodwill." He even found it at a wedding.

There's going to be a wedding *soon*.

The window is willing to let go of its winter's hold, but I am still clinging to mine. I'm still suspicious of finding goodwill out beyond the confines of what I know in my own heart. I should be trusting spring by now, but I am still ambivalent about all this. I haven't even started checking the box scores on the Red Sox yet, and it's six weeks into the baseball season.

The tree has trusted spring, though; I should take it from the tree. The tree that was the last to give in has now found unfrozen ground with which to nourish itself and its leaves are out, not to their full width yet, but out none-theless. I will gather strength from this soon, but not quite yet.

I'm still holding on. Something in me doesn't want to let go of winter. I think I'm afraid of the green. I've trusted in the green before and been disappointed. I'm afraid of the warm air, and the sunshine, and the good times, too. I've gotten ahold of something in this New England winter that I am reluctant to part with. Something real.

Though I will never be a real New Englander (I feel as if I could live here the rest of my life and it still wouldn't be enough), there is one part of life here that I have con-nected with. Having to track with a tree in New England through the dead of winter has led me to a deeper under-standing of my faith. I have found the rooted part, the inner part of my faith that is not connected to anything but my own relationship with God. I think I'm afraid that if I come out, the way these leaves have come out on the tree outside my window, I may soon turn my attention to the green, to the weather, to spring coming and summer on the way, and forget my roots. I don't want to give in to the circum-stances of the seasons and find out in the first chill of au-tumn that my hope has been misplaced again.

Follow the leaf, and the story ends; follow the tree, and it has only begun.

It's easier to forget your roots in spring; in winter in New England, roots are all you have.

There's going to be a wedding soon *in our backyard.*

The yard is buzzing with activity. Friends of the bride and groom are raking, weeding, scraping and painting. I listen to their voices, made louder through the open window, just as I can hear the tree now as well as see it—hear the soft thin rustling of its tender new leaves in the warm wind. With all the racket outside, however, the soft rustling can only be heard in the interludes. Children from the nursery school blend their higher pitches in with all the buzzing. The voices invite me, like a child being called out to play by a best friend.

Some of the brand-new leaves on the maple tree have been spotted with flying paint. My help is getting a little careless. No worry—plenty of leaves to go around. It's a veritable wash of green. The tree is going to be so wide and sweeping this year that I should trim its lower branches, but I can't bring myself to do it. It's an extravagant green that sweeps all the way to the ground like the long train of a wedding gown.

A screen door squeaks and slams and I cannot take it any more. I leave my post by the window and join the "work crew" outside. Some work. Everyone's having too much fun out here to be working. I wouldn't be surprised if the paint on the leaves came from a paint fight. From the looks of the paint splattered on our so-called workers, it has. Our house has never had such attention or such joy.

We are all convinced that there has never been, nor ever will be, a wedding like this one. Kathy's oldest daughter is getting married and they have asked me to do the service. I agreed on one condition: that it would be held outside under a certain tree.

You can get a license for anything in California! Yes, this is what I was told when I tried to get my Peninsula Bible Church ministerial license approved in Massachusetts. There simply was no connection to any major recognized denomination or church body. God knows I'm qualified for this, but try and get the Commonwealth of Massachusetts to recognize that. We're getting around it by having a minister friend of mine solemnize the union and sign the certificate while I perform the actual service. It reminds me of what I gave up, by way of credentials, to blow in the summer winds of the '70s—but that is such a small thing now. I have gained too much in experience to wish for any other road.

The closer I get to this event, the more it seems as if our house was made for this wedding. It's as if we came to New England so we could live here in this house for seven years and get it ready for this grand moment. Such preparations.

All the windows have been cleaned now; the dead, released. I've finally realized this is a time for joy. Weddings and births and Easters. Who can remain inside themselves on any of these occasions? Who can't enter into this? How sad indeed to be so trapped. Imagine someone looking at a lovely bride, flushed and blooming and saying, "Just wait until they've been married for a couple of years—if they make *that*." Who could be so cruel? No. This is a time for joy. This is a time when the ordinary cares and worries of the world have to be set aside for a day or two. This is when we look again at the purpose, the real reasons why we do what we do. This is a festival, and God has always liked a good festival; He was always lining them up for the children of Israel.

A wedding is when the women, rooted as they are, bring forth from the ground their blooming, and the men come down from their distant dreams and dance with the flowers in the garden. This is when the neighbors come and sit on our lawn in white chairs and hear the gospel, the good news, in the context of real earthly joy. This is when those who are long-married touch again its mystery, or feel again the pain of separation. This is when the Bridegroom of Bethlehem calls from heaven, and we catch a glimpse of His grace and a glimpse as well of our white skirts, long and flowing, and waiting. This is when we get a picture of what it can and will be. This is when those who don't believe will have to, if only for a moment.

My computer is turned off now most of the time, and I am outdoors a lot. Everything is almost ready. I may not find my certificate on a sheet of official paper with an official seal, but I am officially alive, and I know I am certified by the Holy Spirit who lives in me to represent His truth to this couple and to the witnesses who will soon gather here.

There's going to be a wedding soon in our backyard *under the full canopy of the maple tree outside my window.*

I'm sitting on the porch next door looking back across the driveway and I cannot see my window for the fullness of the tree. I'm sitting in the chair where I used to sit and chat with Malcolm on warm summer evenings, going over my notes. Soon, Marti will give us the signal that it is time for the men to process. We will come from behind the lilac bushes to the spot under the tree that I have prepared, a section I trimmed after all, making an awning for the wedding party to stand under. The bride will come through the arbor for the long walk across the lawn.

A long walk is good. Nothing about this ceremony will be too long. But I want to stretch it all out—make it last, like my hopes for the marriage. I am more hopeful about marriages in general these days, as my own stretches and strains, and I am hopeful too about this one. They are young, but very serious about their commitment. They're doing this right, right down to the traditional wedding vows. The bride wants it all traditional. No loosey-goosey laid-back California style. This is not California, and I look out from Malcolm's screened-in porch at the lush green, the gathering white cumulus clouds, and our white clapboard house all painted and gleaming and remind myself that this is definitely a northeast day.

My mind runs to the song that my friend and I wrote my first year here:

Life is old, winters are cold,
Minds are made up, blinds are down,
New ideas meet with a frown.
But ties are strong here, and we've been drawn here.
There's something for us and something for them,
Here in New England.

The patriot's fame isn't a game.
The blood that was shed on neighboring hills,
Still paints them red when autumn chills.
The flag is respected and we are indebted.
There's something for us and something for them,
Here in New England.

Pacific blue is another hue,
But the frozen sunlight shines
On whitened walls of older times.
Our faith is young here,
Our song is unsung here.
But there's something for us and something for them,
Here in New England.

I think of how our faith is no longer unsung here, but
how it is still young and how it will always be a young faith
if we keep living this way—pushing out to the edges of our
faith and choosing to own what we believe. I think, too, of
all that has been here for me—the loneliness, the doubts,
the challenges, the relationships with those so different
from me. I never did get to play on anyone's team. John
and Phillip are not here today.

Peter would have been here, though, were he still alive.
He undoubtedly would have stopped by many times during the preparations as well and offered timely advice. I
miss his obnoxious voice. To have learned to love and appreciate someone like Peter is to have learned much.

Chuck and Debbie will not be at the wedding. Their
oldest daughter is graduating in an hour at the high school.
Debbie is helping though, by providing a place for the men
to change. She is also providing this porch and comes out

and checks on me from time to time. Chuck, I'm sure, is happy to have one less ceremony to attend. The last time I saw him in a suit was at Alcena's memorial service. They never did have a service for Malcolm, which was the way he wanted it.

Suddenly I am reminded of the Christmas Eve services that became a kind of new tradition for us. They always ended in a candlelight service and then our family and Debbie's would walk home keeping our candles lit the whole way. With them, we would set fire to the logs in our fireplace that were ready and waiting to receive the flame. We had to do it this way—to light the fire from the candle that was first lit in the church, received from candle to candle all the way back to the first light burning on the Advent wreath: from Advent wreath to living room fire; from spiritual fire to home-fire burning. This light always started our Christmas hope.

I remember the year the wind was so cold and strong that we all had to huddle tightly to keep the flame from going out—slowly inching our way against the storm, lighting and relighting from whoever had their flame still burning. It will long be in my memory—such a picture of New England faith—that small mass of humanity creeping slowly along in the night shielding a frail flickering glow that would soon turn into a blaze of yellow warmth in the living room.

Memories like this flood my mind as I look for the wave from Marti that will signal the wedding's start.

A large number of guests are friends Marti has gained from her involvement in the community. She is amazing at this. I swear, for Marti, it's spring all the time. She is always out, always waving in the wind. Marti has been a major part of the *something for them* of my New England song; I have been too into my own lessons in this season. Around here, with only a few exceptions, I am known as Marti Fischer's husband. I am proud of this, and proud to be bringing the truth today to a group of people that my wife has cared for and gathered in our backyard.

I look eagerly for her to wave from our back porch now: it's time for the men to begin processing. There is something so right about all this. Marti will momentarily signal the culmination of months of work, the bulk of which she has planned and energized. Like the "real New England Christmas party" she arranged at our house, I often don't see the significance of these events until they are upon us. Now I see the full impact of all she has gathered and prepared for this day, and I'm honored and humbled to walk into it. I feel a bit like a patriarch.

Maybe this is the way Jacob felt that morning, looking out across the ford of the Jabbok River, his arms and wrists still burning from their twisting and his hip aflame from the socket, but his heart leaping in full possession of his own blessing. He was watching the slow, steady procession of his family and possessions, fording the river below, and he knew he was heading back to the land of his father, a different man entirely from the one who ran in fear so many years earlier. He was ready now. Ready for anything—Esau? Who's Esau, when you have just wrestled face-to-face with God and won?

I am ready.

This is a wedding. This is a major life event. Regardless of what happens in their future, this is the public display of two people becoming one for the rest of their lives. There is simply no way you can over-emphasize this day. It is a day which holds significance for me beyond this wedding.

I am ready to walk under the tree and culminate so much of what it has yielded to me about the *something for us* of New England, or more accurately, the *something for me*. In a way, it is my wedding too—a wedding inside myself of my inner faith and its outward expression in my life. I am finally ready for spring. I am ready to spread these leaves again, knowing I am not looking at them for proof of anything. I'm not looking at anything I accomplish as a measure of growth, or for any hope of security in God. Instead, I am looking to the ground for my nourishment, and the sky above for His love, confident that my real life is hid in the sap that flows strong and true through all seasons.

Follow the leaf and the story ends; follow the tree and it has only begun.

All glorious is the princess within her chamber;
her gown is interwoven with gold.
In embroidered garments she is led to the king;
her virgin companions follow her and are brought to you.
They are led in with joy and gladness. . . .

Psalm 45:13–16

The bride is beautiful. I have already seen her in the house, in her glory. She is like a daughter to me, and I know it will be hard for me to get through this service with a clear, unbroken voice. I have decided I will take my time. There is no hurry. We waited seven years for this. I feel, in many ways, just like I felt the first time I drove up to 24 Green Street: My emotions are all pulled tight inside, but this time, my confidence is unshaken.

I think of my own daughter, now a nine-year-old bridesmaid already flush with her blooming, and wonder what tree she will be married under. I know now it will not be this one.

I go over my notes one more time. There is one part I have written out word for word, because I want to be sure and get it right. It is too close to the edge of my own consciousness right now to trust my memory. I don't have this down for myself yet, though I am learning. This is the part I will say to the groom after the teaching—the part where I make everything clear—after I set the standard. This is more the artist speaking:

I fear, Eric, that as I have talked to you I have presented myself as one who knows what he is talking about. That is not true— that is only my pride—the way I want to present myself to you and all these people.

How can you be good at giving yourself up for someone, or something else? How can that ever be done easily? Marti has a saying that she repeats to me often: "Men dream dreams, and yet satisfy themselves with inventions of a smaller sort."

There is not one man here within the sound of my voice who has not failed at this. And yet we look upon you as if to encourage you and give you advice in this moment, not even seeing that as we speak, there is blood on our hands.

But I am here to remind you, and remind us all, that there is no more blood on the cross. The price has been paid for our forgiveness. This does not give us an excuse to sin, but it gives us the freedom to come out of hiding.

Do I stand on this side, facing you as if only to instruct you? No longer. I will now turn and stand with you as we all three face the example of Christ and pray together. . . .

So we turned, and with our backs to the guests and our faces toward the sturdy black trunk of the maple tree, I prayed under the cover of outstretched arms, next to our house on 24 Green Street, across from the place they call the Green, in the town of Newbury, Massachusetts, a state in what is commonly called New England. Stood under this tree, for one of the last times.